Understanding Pathological Demand Avoidance Syndrome in Children

A Guide for Parents, Teachers and Other Professionals

Phil Christie, Margaret Duncan,

Ruth Fidler and Zara Healy

Jessica Kingsley *Publishers*
London and Philadelphia

First published in 2012
by Jessica Kingsley Publishers
73 Collier Street
London N1 9BE, UK
and
400 Market Street, Suite 400
Philadelphia, PA 19106, USA

www.jkp.com

Library of Congress Cataloging in Publication Data
Understanding pathological demand avoidance syndrome in children : a guide for parents, teachers, and other professionals / Phil Christie ... [et al.].
      p. ; cm. -- (JKP essentials)
  Includes bibliographical references and index.
  ISBN 978-1-84905-074-6 (alk. paper)
  1. Behavior disorders in children. 2. Emotional problems of children. 3. Problem children--Mental health. I. Christie, Phil. II. Series: JKP essentials.
  [DNLM: 1. Child Development Disorders, Pervasive--rehabilitation. 2. Adaptation, Psychological. 3. Adolescent. 4. Child. 5. Social Support. WS 350]
  RJ506.B44U56 2012
  618.92'89--dc22
                              2011009142

British Library Cataloguing in Publication Data
A CIP catalogue record for this book is available from the British Library

ISBN 978 1 84905 074 6

Printed and bound in Great Britain

Understanding Pathological Demand Avoidance Syndrome in Children

CONTENTS

ACKNOWLEDGEMENTS

We would like to acknowledge the enormous contribution made to our understanding of PDA by Elizabeth Newson, whose first clinical accounts illustrated the characteristics and profile of PDA so cogently. Her enthusiasm and determination encouraged others to recognise the distinct needs of these children and inspired us all.

A big thank you to the parents and all the members of the PDA Contact Group forum who have shared their experiences and stories and without whom we'd be less wise.

We would like to recognise the contribution made, directly or otherwise, by the many children we have met and worked with who have challenged our preconceptions and increased our insight. We would also like to thank colleagues at Sutherland House School and Nottingham Regional Society for Adults and Children with Autism (NORSACA) who have given us examples of their work and practice and shared their ideas with us over many years. We are especially grateful to those pupils who have given us permission for their illustrations to be used in Chapter 5.

Thanks are also due to our own families for their encouragement, support and patience.

INTRODUCTION

This book is mainly intended for parents of children with Pathological Demand Avoidance syndrome and those 'front line' professionals, such as teachers, teaching assistants or residential care workers, who find that they come into day-to-day contact with such children. It will also be relevant to other professionals who support children and families in different ways.

The book is a collaborative effort between professionals, with experience in both diagnostic assessment and teaching, and parents who experience the practical and emotional challenge of bringing up their child in a world that is often not understanding or supportive.

The syndrome of PDA was first described in the 1980s by Professor Elizabeth Newson, who at that time was based at the Child Development Research Unit at Nottingham University. The book draws on material that has been produced by Newson and her colleagues over the past 30 years in order to refine our understanding of the condition and how children with this profile can best be supported. These colleagues have included other psychologists and teachers within NORSACA; based either at the diagnostic centre (now named the Elizabeth Newson Centre) or Sutherland House School (a specialist school for children on the autism spectrum) in Nottingham. This material is supplemented and extended by many examples from classroom staff and parents giving their own individual accounts and experiences. Critical to this has been the input from parents who are members of the PDA Contact Group, a national parent group set up in 1997 to provide information and support.

The book outlines our current understanding of PDA and how this relates to other conditions. It aims to amplify this with many descriptions of how the profile is shown in the development and lives of individual children and their families. It is intended to be practical and put forward thoughts, ideas and suggestions that correspond to the multitude of questions that we get from parents and professionals about how they might best deal with their own particular experiences and issues. Often there aren't definitive 'answers' as each child and situation is unique. It's more a question of trying to develop an understanding and insight into the way that children with PDA approach the world and, in particular, their anxiety-driven need to be in control and avoid other people's demands and expectations. With this understanding, and the examples and strategies drawn from others' experiences, we hope that readers can become more practised at adapting their approach to these children so that it lessens their anxiety and helps them become more tolerant and resilient.

Throughout the book we have used practical examples and case studies based around our clinical and educational experience, as well as those from families that have given accounts through the PDA Contact Group. We are extremely grateful to all those who have provided this supporting material. Names and personal details have, though, been changed to protect confidentiality.

In line with convention we have referred to the child or young person with PDA as he, unless giving a specific example.

In many instances we have referred to the parents of the child with PDA and mean this term to cover both parents and carers.

Chapter 1

WHAT IS PDA?

PATHOLOGICAL DEMAND AVOIDANCE SYNDROME – A BRIEF HISTORY

The term Pathological Demand Avoidance syndrome (PDA) was first used during the 1980s by Professor Elizabeth Newson. The initial descriptions were introduced in a series of lectures, presentations and papers that described a gradually developing understanding of a group of children who had been referred for diagnostic assessment at the clinic based at the Child Development Research Unit at Nottingham University. This clinic operated as part of a centre for postgraduate training of clinical and educational psychologists and had a specialism in children who had communication and developmental difficulties. Most of the children referred were very complex in their development, and many reminded the referring professionals of children with autism or Asperger's syndrome. At the same time, though, they were often seen as not being typical of either of these diagnostic profiles.

Newson and her colleagues began to feel increasingly dissatisfied with the description of 'atypical autism', which was frequently used in the UK at that time. In the USA pervasive developmental disorder not otherwise specified (PDD-NOS) was the term used to mean the same. They felt that it was unhelpful to parents to be told that their child was not typical of a particular condition. Neither was it useful in removing the confusion that was often felt by those who were struggling to gain greater insight into their child's behaviour. Over time, Newson began to notice that while these children were indeed atypical of the clinical picture of autism or Asperger's syndrome they were *typical of each other* in some very important ways. The central feature that was characteristic of all the children was 'an obsessional avoidance of the ordinary demands of everyday life' (Newson 1990, p.1; see also Newson, Le Marechal and David 2003). This was combined with sufficient social understanding and sociability to enable the child to be 'socially manipulative' in their avoidance. It was this level of social understanding, along with a capacity for imaginative play, which most strongly countered a diagnosis of autism.

Through a series of publications, based on increasingly large groups of children (up to 150 cases) and supported by follow-up studies (Newson and David 1999), the clinical description of PDA was refined and the differences between this profile and those found in children with a diagnosis of autism or Asperger's syndrome made clearer (Newson 1996; Newson and Le Marechal 1998). The studies also demonstrated the robustness of the clinical descriptions from childhood into adulthood. These publications culminated in a proposal (Newson *et al.* 2003) to recognise PDA as 'a separate entity within the pervasive developmental disorders' (p.595). Newson proposed that the clinical description of PDA be conceptualised as a separate identity as it gives 'specific status to a large proportion of those children and adults who earlier might have been diagnosed as having pervasive developmental disorder not otherwise specified' (p.595), a much less helpful diagnosis in terms of guidelines for intervention.

DEFINING CRITERIA FOR DIAGNOSIS OF PATHOLOGICAL DEMAND AVOIDANCE SYNDROME

1. Passive early history in the first year.

2. Continues to resist and avoid ordinary demands of life...strategies of avoidance are essentially socially manipulative.

3. Surface sociability, but apparent lack of sense of social identity, pride or shame.

4. Lability of mood, impulsive, led by need to control.

5. Comfortable in role play and pretending.

6. Language delay, seems the result of passivity: good degree of catch-up.

7. Obsessive behaviour.

8. Neurological involvement.

Newson *et al.* (2003)

DIAGNOSIS AND CLASSIFICATION

The publications on PDA have attracted great interest and a degree of controversy. The overriding reason for this interest has been the strong sense of recognition expressed by both parents and professionals of the behavioural profile so cogently described. One parent wrote to the centre saying:

It was a huge consolation to find a set of characteristics and criteria that seemed to have been made for my child...after years of reluctant trawling through ASD diagnostic criteria and really feeling that something didn't sit right, here was a tailor-made paper on my child.

The controversy that exists, particularly among the medical community, has been about whether PDA does exist as a separate syndrome within the pervasive developmental disorders or whether the behaviours described are part of the autism spectrum.

The area of classification, categorisation and diagnosis is complex and variable, with a range of views and models put forward by various professional groups and individuals. As stated, Newson initially proposed PDA as a separate syndrome within the pervasive developmental disorders, which is the recognised category used within the psychiatric classification systems put forward by the World Health Organization (1992: ICD-10) and the American Psychiatric Association (1994: DSM-IV). Autism and Asperger's syndrome appear as diagnosable disorders within this category, as do pervasive developmental disorder not otherwise specified (DSM-IV) and atypical autism (ICD-10). Newson concluded that PDA is a separate entity as the sample demonstrated that the identified children had the pattern of features in common and that these features could be significantly differentiated from those with other syndromes, namely autism and Asperger's syndrome.

Diagnostic systems and categories, though, as well as showing variation in the way they are used by different professional groups or individuals, are also evolving and developing concepts. DSM-5, for example, will be published in May 2013. Newson recognised this when devising a diagram (Newson 1999) to demonstrate how she thought of PDA as a specific disorder that, along with other disorders including autism and Asperger's syndrome, makes up the 'family' of disorders known as pervasive developmental disorders (see Figure 1.1). The diagram shows 'clusters of symptoms' (syndromes) that represent specific disorders within the pervasive developmental disorders. Newson saw PDA as a separate syndrome related to autism and Asperger's syndrome and pointed out that there may be some children who fall between these 'typical clusters' (i.e. they share characteristics of both syndromes). The caption for this diagram of the family of pervasive developmental disorders includes the note: *sometimes 'autistic spectrum' is loosely used to describe the* whole *family*. In adding this Newson foresaw what has subsequently taken place.

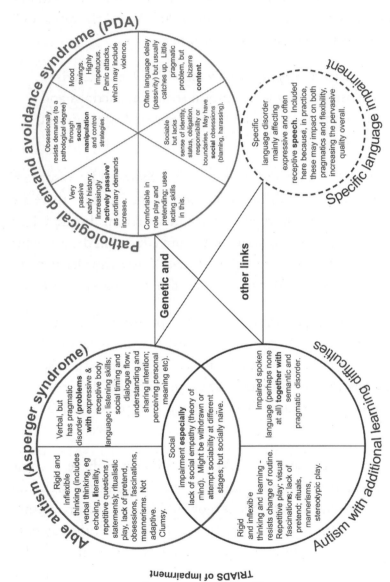

Figure 1.1 The family of pervasive developmental disorders (sometimes 'autistic spectrum' is loosely used to described the whole family) (Newson 1999)

Over the last few years the term autistic (or autism) spectrum disorder (ASD) has become increasingly used to cover the range of individuals showing the qualitative differences in social interaction, communication and the ability to think flexibly that make up what is known as the 'triad of impairments'. In the UK the National Autism Plan for Children (National Initiative for Autism: Screening and Assessment 2003) used the term ASD throughout its report with the following meaning:

> the group of *pervasive developmental disorders* (PDD) characterised by qualitative abnormalities in reciprocal social interactions and in patterns of communication, and by a restricted, stereotyped repertoire of interests and activities. (p.15)

It is also the case that the spectrum is now usually followed by 'disorders' (with deliberate use of the plural) in recognition of the fact that there are almost certainly a number of subtypes within the spectrum. In the UK, a governmental working group across the health and education departments published *Autistic Spectrum Disorders: Good Practice Guidance* (Department for Education and Skills and Department of Health 2002) and pointed to:

> a number of sub-groups within the autistic spectrum. There are differences between the sub-groups and further work is required on defining the criteria… It may be necessary to adopt specific strategies in relation to particular areas of difficulty in order to assist a child to maximise their potential and preserve their dignity. (p.6)

It seems that, in practice, the terms ASD and PDD may have become synonymous. Indeed, the National Autism Plan for Children went on to say that autism spectrum disorder is not in itself a category within medical diagnostic systems but that it 'broadly coincides with the category of pervasive developmental disorder' (p.74). The National Institute for Health and Clinical Excellence, in its *Scope for Consultation on 'Autism Spectrum Disorders in Children and Young People'* (2009) used the term ASD throughout its guidance 'instead of PDD because it is more widely understood'. The proposed revision for DSM-5 (2010) suggests that autism spectrum disorder becomes the new name for the category and that the term should include autism, Asperger's syndrome and pervasive developmental disorder not otherwise specified.

With these changes in definition and terminology PDA is increasingly being recognised as part of the autism spectrum, and this has been reflected in the recent updating of information on the National Autistic Society website (www.autism.org.uk).

In this context, it has already been argued (Christie 2007) that prolonged debate about whether PDA is a syndrome within the family of pervasive developmental disorders, or a sub-group of what has become another umbrella term of autism spectrum disorders, becomes a distraction. Instead, we should be focused on the true purpose of diagnosis: to better understand and make sense of individuals and to use that understanding to help us formulate more effective forms of intervention and provision.

PATHOLOGICAL DEMAND AVOIDANCE SYNDROME – THE KEY FEATURES

In the remaining part of this chapter we want to describe in more detail the key features of PDA, by taking each of the criteria that Elizabeth Newson listed in turn (see box on p.13). As further research takes place, and our understanding of PDA is refined, it is likely to be the case that the original list of criteria will be reduced. This will distinguish those criteria that are *essential* for a diagnosis, from those that are commonly associated but not necessarily found in all children. This is a similar process to that which took place in earlier formulations of autism, when longer lists of symptoms were reduced to the three features contained within the 'triad of impairments' which came to be seen as essential for a diagnosis.

Throughout both this chapter, and subsequent ones, examples have been given which are taken from a variety of sources. Some have come from reports produced in connection with children seen for a diagnostic assessment at the Elizabeth Newson Centre. These assessments comprise several hours of play-based assessment, where the child and a psychologist are together in a large well-equipped playroom while a consultant psychologist, parents and other professionals observe together. The assessment reports include detailed observations of the child, a comprehensive history from discussion with the parents and a range information provided by school staff and other involved professionals. Other examples come from reports and observations from staff at Sutherland House School, a specialist provision for children across the autism spectrum. Further descriptions have been supplied by parents and have been provided through the PDA Contact Group. In all cases the names of individuals have been changed.

It should be recognised at this point that PDA, like other autism spectrum disorders, is 'dimensional' in nature. This means that the degree and extent of the condition varies in severity and the extent to which it affects individual children. Children with PDA can also be very variable themselves in how they appear at different times, with different people and in various settings. Their threshold for accepting social demands can fluctuate and the factors that influence this are discussed in the next chapter. As with any other children they also show individual pathways in their development due to their own personality, circumstances and life experiences.

1. Passive early history in the first year

Newson's studies found that a high proportion of children with PDA were described by their parents as passive or placid in the first year of their life. Nearly half of the children were said not reach for their toys or to drop them when they were offered. The child, though, begins to become more actively resistant as more is expected of him; some, though, are resistant from the start. Parents frequently report that they adapted so much to their child (often using phrases like 'she needed velvet gloves') that they were unprepared for their later difficulties. These are often highlighted once the child starts in a group setting, such as a nursery with specific demands. Early on in their development children with PDA may be seen as puzzling in some way but not necessarily to have significant difficulties in their development. As a result, initial concerns and diagnosis are often late when compared to children who have autism. While this passive nature is typical of a large group of children who have a diagnosis of PDA, it is by no means universal and should not be seen as essential to the diagnosis.

2. Continues to resist and avoid ordinary demands of life… strategies of avoidance are essentially socially manipulative

This is the feature of behaviour that defines and gives name to the syndrome – *PDA is best understood as an anxiety-driven need to be in control and avoid other people's demands and expectations*. Children can seem under an extraordinary degree of pressure from ordinary everyday demands and expectations and they may attempt to avoid these to a remarkable extent. Demands might include a suggestion that it's time to get up, go out of the house or join a family activity. At times *any* suggestion made by another person can be perceived as a demand. Underpinning this avoidance is an often extreme anxiety about conforming to social demands (which might include requests, suggestions or offers of assistance) and of not being in control of the situation themselves.

Callum's parents described how, at six years old, he wouldn't co-operate with simple day-to-day tasks such as getting dressed and feeding himself. He wouldn't eat unless his parent made deals with him, such as time on the computer for eating his meal. Even then he would often require spoon feeding. The smallest of demands would initiate 'avoidance mode' and he spent a huge amount of time and energy fighting off the demand, when a fraction of that time and energy would have accomplished the request.

Callum would offer an 'escalating amount of resistance'. Initially he would giggle, tease and run away. If his parents weren't distracted the resistance would become more definite and he might offer excuses such as 'I'm busy…I'll do it in a minute…I want to do this first.' His next level would be to say 'I feel sick…my tummy hurts' and so on. He would give reasons such as it's too hard, too stiff or too heavy. If compliance was still pushed then he became upset and tearful, followed by anger, shouting and throwing, finally throwing himself to the floor if the demand was not withdrawn.

At times, this inability to accept situations, unless they have determined the way in which they should take place, can prevent children with PDA from enjoying an experience altogether. One mother described this tellingly when writing to us about her then ten-year-old daughter, Joanna, who has been seen several times both at the centre and in her school.

She will prevent herself from engaging in activities or outings unless the situation is manipulated so that she feels it was her idea. An example of this is when we plan for trips out with the children. I recently purchased some tickets for the pantomime, which Joanna was delighted about. However, when I explained to her that we had been given special seats to ensure that the children could see the performance, and have access to the exit if needed, Joanna became extremely angry and refused to attend, stating that she hated the seats that were selected. Joanna has missed out on several trips where it is obvious that she would love to have gone, but her demand avoidance prevents this from happening. It is very sad to watch Joanna miss out on so much of her life because her avoidance is such a dominant force.

Of course, children with autism may also react to social demands by becoming avoidant, but they tend to do this in an asocial way; ignoring, withdrawing, walking away, etc. A key feature of PDA is that the child has sufficient social understanding and empathy to be socially manipulative in their endeavours and will often adapt strategies to the person making the demand. 'Manipulative' is a term which some people dislike and it can have negative connotations. It was, though, deliberately chosen to describe the fact that not only are children with PDA motivated to avoid demands but they are successful because they have sufficient social empathy to do so. Parents very often use the term 'manipulative' to describe this aspect of their child's behaviour and will often comment on how it seems to be their greatest skill. Often they will make a remark like 'If only they would put half the effort in to doing what it was I wanted as they do to getting out of it.'

When Oscar was just under five years old his dad described him as the 'master manipulator' who was able to manage his parents, other adults and his younger brother. He went on to describe how he continually bombards them with ideas and suggestions in order to avoid getting down to anything: 'He might say "I know, let's play cars" or "Let's go to Granny's" and then "No, no just do X or Y"…until he's worn you into submission.'

Children may use a wide range of strategies that might include distraction, giving excuses, delaying, saying that they can't, arguing, suggesting alternatives and withdrawing into fantasy. During a recent assessment, one five-year-old child gave responses which included:

No... I can't... I'll be there in ten minutes... Look, Jenny! I don't know... I think I'm done... I can't do it, I told you, I'm grumpy... I want to be a policeman... I'm going to tell my mum and dad... I hate putting this away... A bit later... You play with those, I'll be in my castle... I'll come back when I'm ready... I've run out of energy... No! That's not my game. I want to go now... I don't trust you... I'm waiting for my family... I'm not a child.

A letter from a paediatrician, referring another five-year-old, to the centre stated:

He has a wide variety of strategies to avoid obeying direct demands. He acts as if he hasn't heard, carrying on with what he's doing with a blank expression on his face. He distracts by starting to talk about something else and he will go on and on until his mother has forgotten what she wanted him to do. He makes excuses such as 'I've just got to...' He says 'I can't' in a plaintive voice or falls to the floor and starts rolling around like a baby.

Heather came to the centre when she was seven years old, described as a child with an autism spectrum disorder but, according to her teacher, with 'avoidance as the biggest barrier to her learning'. Heather also had a long-standing interest in role play and in acting out characters from TV. The following extract is taken from the observational report that contributed to her assessment.

Throughout the assessment Heather tended to be avoidant when Georgina suggested activities that involved her having to sit down at the table, and used a number of different strategies to avoid doing as she had been asked to. These included making excuses as to why she couldn't sit down, distracting Georgina by saying that Sam the Monkey was laughing at her, saying that something was too difficult for her or by removing herself from the situation by going into the playhouse. On many occasions Heather used imaginary play in order to avoid taking part in activities that Georgina suggested. For example, she declined a request by saying 'No thank you, let's have our picnic now'. Later on she said she needed to go and put the dressing up clothes away when she was asked to complete the creative colour cubes cards. When Georgina said that she could do this later, she replied that she couldn't as she would be having her picnic then.

Children with PDA will often give reasons or explanations why they can't do something that they have been asked, having sufficient social empathy to realise that a response is expected. Often, though, the explanation they give is completely fictitious. Remarks such as 'my legs don't work', 'I can't do it…my hands are flat' and 'I can't talk… I'm a statue' have all been made by children during assessments at the centre. Ronan's parents described the feeling of 'endless negotiations' of this sort that can occur with him over everyday tasks. For example, 'If asked to put his shoes on, he makes excuses such as "I don't know where my shoes are" and when told they are in the hall "I don't know where the hall is". If then given his shoes, he will say "I can't put them on my feet – I can't close them".' This sort of extended exchange can be incredibly wearing for those living and working with children who have PDA.

As well as these strategies that demonstrate a degree of social under-standing that would be unusual in children with other autism spectrum difficulties, children with PDA may also use straightforward refusal or outbursts of explosive behaviour including violence. It is best to see these explosions as a form of panic on the part of the child. It is usually when other strategies haven't worked or when their anxiety is too high and their tolerance too low, that they will 'explode' or have a 'meltdown'. This can take the form of shouting, screaming, throwing things and physically lashing out, often in very sudden and dramatic ways. Mikey's mum described how bedtimes were always really difficult for him and the family and didn't improve until he was about eight or nine.

For Mikey the whole process seemed like a series of demands. Getting clothes off, getting pyjamas on, taking medication, brushing teeth, getting washed, etc. Sometimes we would get as far as trying to get his clothes off and then come to a stand off. If I persisted in asking him, his face would get angrier and angrier and he'd start shouting 'NO!' or 'I don't want to' then he'd start throwing things in his room at me and screaming. This could last for an hour or longer. If I tried to leave he would scream at me in panic not to leave, yet if I stayed he would continue to hit or punch out and throw things. Often he'd just burn himself out and end up falling asleep with his clothes still on. This would happen two or three times a week sometimes.

As with any other features of behaviour these sorts of outbursts need to be seen within the context of the child's overall development. Explosive outbursts are not uncommon in two- or three-year-olds, for a whole range of reasons, but become much less typical, as well as less appropriate and more difficult to manage, if they persist later on into childhood. Not all children with PDA have explosive outbursts, but it seems to affect a significant number, with Newson reporting extreme outbursts in 60 per cent in her study. When it is coupled with impulsivity and difficulties in recognising the consequences of their behaviour it can become exceptionally challenging to manage both at home and school. Advice on how to handle these situations is discussed in more detail later in the book.

3. Surface sociability, but apparent lack of sense of social identity, pride or shame

Children with PDA tend to be very 'people-orientated', if only because they are alert to what might be asked of them. They have usually learnt many social niceties and may decline a request or suggestion with 'No, thank you', 'I'm very sorry but...' or 'Do you mind if...?'. A number will use charm in their repertoire of avoidance tactics if this has proven to be effective on past occasions. They can often seem exceptionally well tuned in to what might prove effective as a strategy with particular people. It was this apparently well-developed social understanding and empathy, along with comparatively good eye-contact and body language, which was first observed by Newson. These were the main features which made the children in the first descriptions of PDA seem unlike those with autism. However, the sociability tends to be skin deep and the child may be very misleading in this respect. Their social approaches and responses can be unsubtle and without depth, as though they know that a response is required but are unsure at what level. This can lead, for example, to children being overpowering in their responses, overreacting to seemingly trivial events or become domineering in the way they try to organise others.

When Andrew was seen at the centre, aged six, his parents described how he had always been sociable with other people but that they were worried that he was rather indiscriminate in his reactions to people, particularly in the way he would 'go to anyone'. He tends to want to instruct or command other people, but in contrast can be 'over polite'. He also might overemphasise the significance of something and, for example, say in a very serious way 'I'm sorry to have to tell you…' but then go on to talk about a very trivial event.

A feature of this poor judgement is an ambiguity in their mood and responses so that, for example, hugging becomes pinching and they may embrace their parent while saying 'I hate you'. One child arrived at the centre with a beaming smile and asked excitedly, 'Have you got any fish?' When he was told that there was an aquarium in the next room, and asked if he would like to see them, he changed dramatically and ran away squealing, 'No… I hate fish.' This ambiguity is also reflected in the way that many children will respond to praise by insisting that it's not meant or by destroying the work that you have just commented on. This sort of behaviour demonstrates both their own confusion and the fact that their behaviour can be confusing to others.

The degree of social empathy (the capacity to understand and share what another person is thinking and feeling) present in children with PDA is especially significant. On the surface it seems much better developed than would be expected in other children on the spectrum and is certainly sufficient to be able to use the sort of socially controlling strategies that have been described. In most cases, though, there is a feeling that this too is only skin deep and that there is a marked difference in being able to empathise at an *intellectual* level as opposed to an *emotional* one. Children with PDA may be comparatively skilled in working out and knowing that a particular behaviour or attribute may have a specific outcome with an individual. They may have the vocabulary to describe people's reactions or emotions within a scenario that they see depicted during an assessment. They are much less likely though to be able to experience this at an emotional level and fully understand and share what another person is feeling.

Andrew's parents went on to describe how Andrew had been watching some of the news coverage of the tsunami disaster which showed a little girl who had lost her parents. Andrew commented 'that's very sad…the little girl has lost her mummy and daddy'. He then went on to explain what he would do if this happened to him by saying 'I'd leave home…there wouldn't be any point in staying'.

One clinical psychologist in her report about a ten-year-old boy who was later seen for assessment at the centre wrote about him that, 'although he has an intellectual understanding of social rules and is able to see how these might apply to others, he shows no motivation to apply them to himself and appears unable to establish an emotional empathy for others'.

Figure 1.2 depicts three different levels of social empathy. The first involves *recognising* someone else's emotional state from the situation they are in, what they say or how they behave. The second is about *sharing* some of that emotion through a process of contagion (e.g. feeling excited about an event because of the reactions of those around you). The third is *modifying* your own action to accommodate someone else's needs. Most children with PDA are comparatively good at recognition but find making accommodations and sharing emotions much harder.

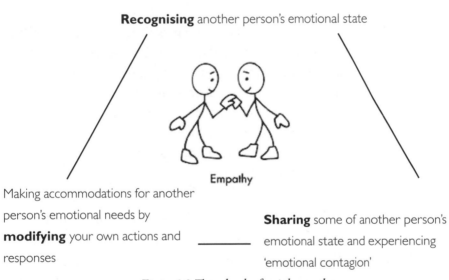

Recognising another person's emotional state

Empathy

Making accommodations for another person's emotional needs by **modifying** your own actions and responses

Sharing some of another person's emotional state and experiencing 'emotional contagion'

Figure 1.2 Three levels of social empathy

Newson felt that at the heart of PDA was an enormous difficulty for the child in developing a sense of what she described as 'personal identity'. One example of this is the way in which the child fails to identify with other children as a group and more naturally gravitates towards adults. During the parental interviews that are part of the diagnostic assessment, parents are often asked the question 'Do you think he knows that he's a child?'. At first this seems an extremely unusual question to ask but many parents quickly show a sense of recognition and respond along the lines of 'I hadn't thought about it quite like that…but you're right, he seems to think he's got the same rights as an adult'.

One parent described their 12-year-old son by saying: 'To other children he will happily act as if he were their mother "Have you washed your hands?… Don't put your elbows on the table"…but doesn't have a sense of himself also needing to follow basic table manners.'

Edward's parents talked about how he treats everyone the same. 'He's got no sense of authority and doesn't recognise "a pecking order". He generally relates well to adults and responds better if you adopt an adult style of speech to him. He talks to other children as though he was an adult or in a teacher role and, for example, will try to stop children going out to play if it's raining. He treats his sister in the same way as his parents do, as though he was just another adult.'

Josh has told his parents that he is 'a short adult'. From an early age he has shown a strong preference for being with adults, and the staff at his nursery commented: 'Josh likes to take on adult roles whilst in the nursery and finds if very hard to interact at an appropriate age level with his peers. He regularly states that he is a 63-year-old with six children and his "occupation" changes every couple of days.' Furthermore, 'He states himself that he is an adult not a child.' He would write a list of children in the pre-school group and the staff which worked with them and would include his name with the adults.

As a consequence of all this, children with PDA often fail to understand many of the unwritten social boundaries or divides that exist, say between adults and children. This can mean that they become over-familiar or bossy with an adult in inappropriate ways. They seem to lack a sense of pride or embarrassment and can behave in very uninhibited ways that are out of keeping with their age and pay little attention to the attempts of adults to appeal to their 'better nature'. It also means that they have a difficulty in accepting social obligation and taking responsibility for their own actions and behaviour.

Karl's mother felt that he seemed to have no idea what it is to be naughty, although other people regard him as such. He still, at five, seems to have no boundaries. She feels that she exerts the ordinary boundaries but that Karl simply doesn't recognise them as applying to him, and will constantly try to get past them. If he is in a tantrum, it would make no difference to point it out to him that someone is watching, whereas his younger sister would become shy and embarrassed in that situation. Similarly, he is not ashamed of still messing his pants, he doesn't hide what is happening and would do it in front of his mother.

All of this means that children with PDA find making successful relationships with other children especially difficult. They are usually very interested in other children and want to have friends but find that others are often shocked and confused by their behaviour. Children with PDA often get relationships wrong through their misjudged approaches and their need to control other children who are generally much less able, or prepared, to organise some form of negotiation than an adult. They may also blame other children for things that have gone wrong, even if it is attributable to their own behaviour.

4. Lability of mood, impulsive, led by need to control

Children with PDA can characteristically switch from one mood to another very suddenly (e.g. from happy and content to distraught) in a way that parents describe as 'like switching a light on and off'. One father described this by saying of his son, 'He can go from 0 to 90 faster than any car in existence – and from 90 to 0 at the same speed.' The emotions shown in this sort of situation may seem very dramatic and 'over the top' or, according to some parents 'like an act'.

Edward's parents described how he finds understanding and managing his emotions very difficult. If they start to get upset with him he still keeps pushing regardless. He can also lose control of his own temper very quickly and then 'get over it in an instant'. His parents gave an example of him getting into a real rage at school and, in an attempt to distract him, the head teacher asked 'Would you like to come and see a play?' Edward stopped almost instantly, saying 'Oh…yes please!'

Difficulty with regulating emotions is common in children with autism spectrum disorders, but seems especially prevalent in PDA. One of Newson's studies compared the profiles of 50 children with PDA with a similar number of children with 'classical autism' and Asperger's syndrome. Excessive lability (or changing) of mood (found in 68% of the PDA group) was one of the behavioural features that clearly discriminated between the groups. Mood swings and impulsivity, where a child or young person seems driven to follow an impulse in a very impetuous way, were also shown to persist beyond childhood in the majority of those with PDA. This switching of moods is linked to the social ambiguity described above and very often seems to be driven by the child's needs to be in control. Frequently the child may invite a suggestion on the part of an adult only then to reject it angrily in order to regain control. Newson *et al.* (2000, p.11) gave an example which illustrates this perfectly.

Mother:	Would you like Smarties or chocolate buttons?
Ross:	Which do *you* think I should have?
Mother:	Smarties?
Ross (shrieks):	Oh no, no, no, I don't want Smarties!
Mother:	Well, have whichever you want then.
Ross (calm again):	Which do *you* think I should have?
Mother:	Chocolate buttons?
Ross (shrieks):	Oh no, no, no, no, I don't want…

Rapid and often unexpected changes of moods, together with their overall variability of behaviour, makes children with PDA very unpredictable and wearing to be with. Many parents and teachers will describe this feeling as though 'you are always walking on eggshells'.

5. Comfortable in role play and pretending

Children with PDA are often highly interested in role play and pretend. This, along with their level of social understanding, was recognised early on as being untypical of children with autism. These characteristics made them stand out from others on the spectrum. Children with PDA often mimic and take on the roles of others, extending and taking on their style, not simply repeating and re-enacting what they may have heard or seen in a repetitive or echoed way. About a third of children in Newson's studies were reported to confuse reality and pretence at times.

Since Charlotte was very young she was a 'little actress', often pretending to be the teacher and being a very good mimic. Charlotte uses quite a lot of fantasy in general and will make up 'fantastic stories' almost as if they are true. Her parents described overhearing her on the phone to her grandmother saying 'I haven't been to school today… I've been vomiting all day'. She might tell a stranger that they live on a farm or that they're going to Australia. When they point these things out to her they think she's aware that it's not true but doesn't think there's anything wrong. They were able to point out an example of this during the assessment. While Charlotte and Anna (Assistant Psychologist) were talking about the 'What's wrong cards', Charlotte started to tell Anna that she had a flute that she enjoyed playing (which is not the case).

Nadine sometimes finds it hard to distinguish fantasy from reality and her parents described how she doesn't seem to understand that dogs aren't human. They overheard her one day taking the dog to one side and saying: 'Now they're not watching you can talk to me.'

As well as being a common area of interest, children with PDA will often incorporate role play or pretend in the strategies that they use to avoid demands or control events and people. When they become involved in play scenarios with other people, they will nearly always try to direct the other person. This can cause real conflict, especially with other children. The next example is an extract from an observational report of Joanna (aged seven at her first assessment at the centre) with Carla (Assistant Psychologist) involved in an episode of doll play. While observing her, mum commented that this was very typical of the way that Joanna would try to play with other children and why she found it hard to maintain friendships.

Carla and Joanna were playing with the doll's house. They chose two dolls each; Joanna placed her dolls in the lounge, and Carla chose to place one of her dolls in the dining room. However, when Carla tried to do this, Joanna would not allow her to do so.

Joanna: No don't…it's not time to eat.

Carla: But she's hungry.

Joanna: Yes, but she can't because the food is raw.

Carla: But she wants a packet of crisps and they can't be raw.

Joanna: Well they're gone off.

Carla: You're right, one packet is gone off, but the other packet I only bought yesterday so she can have that one

Joanna's response to Carla's final comment was to throw both of Carla's dolls across the playroom. When Carla then went to fetch her dolls, she asked Joanna whether she could put one of them in the bathroom to pretend that they were having a bath, but Joanna got very close to Carla, held her dolls up to Carla's face and shouted, 'No… They have to sit on the sofa!', in an aggressive manner.

Themes of pretend play in children can develop around very strong fascinations in some children and for a few can be pursued with an obsessive force that they find hard to break out of by themselves.

Nadine's parents also recounted a stage where she wanted to become a teacher and invented a school called Merrivale. She printed lesson plans, tried to direct Mum and Dad as her pupils, invited people by letter to attend the school (this was when she was on half days at school), and made visitors to the house become her pupils. She set up desks and gave names and badges to her dolls and teddies and would buy exercise books for them. For a time this took Nadine over and she became obsessed and couldn't break out of it. In the end she sent out her own circular saying that Merrivale School is closed.

6. Language delay, seems the result of passivity: good degree of catch-up

The large majority of children with PDA are delayed in some aspect of their early speech and language development, although this may be dependent on their overall intellectual ability. This initial delay seems to be part of their general passivity and there is often a striking and sudden degree of catch-up. Newson reported speech delay in as many as 90 per cent of her sample but with the majority having caught up with expected development by the age of six. Callum, referred to in the earlier example (p.19), was first seen at the centre when aged nearly three and had no functional language, only very limited echoed speech. When he was seen for reassessment shortly after his sixth birthday he was talking in long and complex sentences and his opening comment to the consultant was 'Hello, I can't stay for long, I don't feel well, I'll have to be taken to hospital in an ambulance and have my blood pressure done!'

Children with PDA show more fluent use of eye-contact (other than when avoiding demands) and conversational timing than is the case with children with autism. They tend generally to have less difficulty with the pragmatics of language (those non-verbal aspects which enable language to become communication). Difficulties do though remain for some children, such as taking things literally, and in understanding sarcasm and teasing. The content of what they say is often unusual, often because of the amount of social mimicry and role play used.

Over recent years the opportunity to see increasing numbers of children with PDA for assessment at the Elizabeth Newson Centre has led to a clearer understanding of the pattern of communication in these children. While the majority of children with PDA develop very fluent expressive language, it is the case that some do not have such robust understanding. It is not so much that they do not understand the language that is used (i.e. that they lack the grammatical knowledge), rather that they have difficulty with processing what they hear and the time that it takes them to do this. This, coupled with demand avoidance, can lead to misunderstandings and disruption to the communication process.

We have also been looking in more detail at pragmatic language impairment in children with PDA and routinely use a checklist of skills as part of this process (Children's Communication Checklist: Dorothy Bishop 2003). The profiles demonstrate that despite their verbal fluency, children with PDA often have difficulties in the speed with which they process language, and that their fluency can mask difficulties with their use of language, particularly when they are not in control.

7. Obsessive behaviour

Strong fascinations and special interests which may be pursued to an obsessive degree are, of course, very characteristic of children with autism spectrum disorders. This criterion does not distinguish a child with PDA from those with other ASDs. Newson noted that the demand-avoidant behaviour itself usually has an 'obsessive feel'. Children with PDA may have a strong fascination with pretend characters and scenarios, as mentioned on p.29.

Edward's mother described how he has developed a number of very strong fascinations. His current fascination is with Robot Wars, with which they say he is 'fixated'. When he's following an interest like this, there are times when he does it to the extent of taking on characters. They commented during the observation several times, that his rather awkward gait was because he was taking on the part of a robot. This has happened with other characters too. Edward is 'acting all the time' and on other occasions might be a chicken or a frog.

Often the subjects of fixations for children with PDA tend to be social in nature and often revolve around specific individuals. This can result in blame, victimisation and harassment, which can cause real problems for peer relationships in school. One teacher, writing about Tim, aged five, described how he: 'is very attached to a boy called Adam. He is only interested in emulating Adam's work and often talks to him and ignores the teacher. He will only eat food if he thinks Adam is eating at the same time.'

8. Neurological involvement

Newson included evidence of some neurological involvement in PDA in her original list of criteria but described how this aspect of the condition is under-researched. This remains the case. Studies indicated that crawling was late or absent in more than half of the children concerned and other milestones, such as age of sitting, are delayed in a significant minority. Clumsiness and physical awkwardness are quite common and many were described as 'flitting' in attention, but more that a third of these only showed this behaviour when demands were being made.

OVERLAP, CO-MORBIDITY AND MIS-DIAGNOSIS

In the explanatory notes to the diagram of pervasive developmental disorders (Figure 1.1) Newson described how 'clusters of symptoms' or syndromes were shown and made up specific disorders. She went on to point out that some children will show a pattern that falls between typical clusters, showing features of different sub-groups and perhaps becoming closer to a particular group over time, as particular features assume greater prominence. It is also the case that PDA can co-exist alongside other conditions, such as mental health problems, in the same way as autism or Asperger's syndrome. Sometimes the co-existing condition can take away attention from the underlying core difficulty, which is then overlooked. The diagnostic profiles of various conditions, of course, have many features or criteria that are similar to each other. In order to make a differential diagnosis, the developmental picture as a whole must be considered and a full understanding built up of the child's history over time and his behaviour in different settings and situations. For parents of children with PDA getting an appropriate diagnosis can be extremely difficult, due both to the lack of understanding of the condition and to the possibility of overlaps and co-existing problems. Many parents report a difficult time in their contacts with professionals who don't recognise the nature and extent of their child's difficulties. They often feel blamed, that their child's anxiety isn't taken into account and that their behaviour is regarded as being a result of 'ineffective parenting'. A number have had their child's difficulties wrongly attributed to an attachment disorder, in spite of the fact that there is no evidence of what the DSM describes as 'pathogenic care' (e.g. disregard of the child's basic emotional or physical needs, repeated changes in caregiver or bringing up in 'unusual settings'). Clearly this can have devastating impact on the family as a whole and lead to unhelpful interventions for the child.

WHY DOES A DIAGNOSIS MATTER?

Parents of any child on the autism spectrum, or indeed of almost all children with special educational needs, will come across the tensions that exist between a medical model of diagnosis and categorisation and an educational model that is based on the identification of individual needs.

Some professionals will use the pejorative term 'labelling' to describe the process of diagnosis and parents may feel an implicit criticism for wanting to 'label' their child. Sadly, diagnostic and assessment procedures are quite frequently conducted, and their outcomes communicated, in such a way that parents are left with just this: a label. A diagnosis should engage the parents or carers in such a way that leads to a better understanding of their child and is therefore linked in a logical way to appropriate educational and other interventions or support. The diagnosis should also be concerned with individual strengths as well as areas of need, and should reflect the child's unique profile and personality, together with the way in which they match the criteria for a particular diagnosis. Newson described this procedure as one of 'mapping' and detailed the importance of differential diagnosis, highlighting parental dissatisfaction with the vagueness of general terms such as ASD when applied to individual children.

The experience of families that have been seen at the centre, or been involved with the PDA Contact Group, echoes this feeling. One parent, speaking at a recent conference organised for parents and professionals about PDA, described a common reaction:

The paediatrician did place Daniel on the autistic spectrum but it didn't quite fit – if the hole's big enough, the square peg will fit. We accepted this but then we came across the diagnostic criteria for PDA and this fitted Daniel perfectly. Some people thought it didn't matter if PDA was on Daniel's statement [of special educational needs] but it did to us; it did especially for Daniel, so he could receive the correct input.

It is often said of children with PDA that they are 'complex'; and while this is certainly true, it also reflects the fact that they confuse people and that there is variation in the way that different people understand them and their behaviour. A diagnosis should be about reaching a shared understanding of a child's profile; a formulation that can lead to an agreed way of making sense of his behaviour.

KEY CHARACTERISTICS OF THE CHILD AS LEARNER

As in most specialist schools in the UK, the pupil profile at Sutherland House has become increasingly complex over the past few years. This has included an increase in the number of referrals and admissions of children who fit the PDA profile, most of whom had been in other school placements (both mainstream and special), which had resulted in major breakdown. A number of these children had been out of school for several months; in one case for more than a year. In response to this, a working group of senior managers, teachers, psychologists, therapists and teaching assistants from across the school started to meet regularly to consider the needs of this group of pupils. The purpose of this group was to re-examine and update the existing educational and handling guidelines (Newson 1998) and to share experiences and good practice. This work was supplemented by the wider clinical experience of children referred for diagnostic assessment at the centre, which works in very close collaboration with the school.

An initial focus was to consider the features that these children had in common. The diagnostic criteria were a useful starting point. Certainly the staff were universally faced with the daily challenge of providing for children who were demand avoidant, socially manipulative, impulsive and seemed led by a need to control. The group wanted to look beyond this, though, to the ways in which this impacted on the process of learning and teaching, first looking at the child as a learner and then the adaptations to teaching style and approach that were necessary. These adaptations form the core of Chapter 2.

When considering the child as a learner it is important to remember that not all of the key characteristics, set out below, are present in every child with PDA, the severity of the condition varies as, of course, do other factors such as the individual child's personality, intelligence and interests. *The extent of many of the features will also vary within the same child, according to their mood and circumstances at the time.* The key characteristics we need to consider are:

- need to be in control

- explosive behaviour

- 'slipping under the radar'

- threatening language

- very poor sense of self-esteem

- expressed desire to be equal or better than

- desiring friendships but inadvertently sabotaging them

- ambivalence about success and enjoyment

- lack of permanence and transfer of learning and experience

- very poor emotional regulation

- variability in behaviour

- extensive involvement in fantasy and role play.

Need to be in control

The child often seems to be driven by anxiety and uncertainties. This results in him needing to be in control of the choice of activities, the way in which he does things and of other people's interactions and behaviour. This means that children with PDA can find direction and instruction very difficult and find it hard to compromise or accommodate other people's wishes and needs.

Explosive behaviour

Explosive behaviour may occur when things go wrong. This is because the child cannot accommodate to the demands they feel, or react to them in another more 'adaptive' way (such as asking for help, reassurance or explanation). As highlighted earlier, children with PDA can use a whole range of strategies when faced with what they perceive as a demand. These techniques include distracting people, giving reasons for not doing something or directing other people to behave in the way they would like them to. There will be times for most children, though, if these don't work in the way they expected or their anxiety is too high and their tolerance too low, when they will 'explode' or have a 'meltdown'. This can take the form of shouting, screaming, throwing things and physically lashing out, often in very sudden and dramatic ways.

'Slipping under the radar'

Other children, who have different personalities, are less likely to explode but are very good at 'slipping under the radar', as parents frequently describe it. Sometimes they appear to be more tolerant, or to find ways of fitting in to the learning environment and perhaps creating a sort of 'act' or 'role' of the compliant child. However, they may actually be switching off from processing and absorbing what they appear to be attending to. Parents often feel that their children are not being sufficiently challenged in the content of their lessons and are not learning as well as they might. Alternatively, while not actually being disruptive, children may spend much of their time during lessons 'busy getting nothing done'.

Threatening language

As well as the disruption caused by the explosive behaviour or aggression that may be shown in response to pressure (which can be viewed as a form of panic), the *child may articulate threats* of violence and use obscene and shocking language, which they may have discerned is hard for adults to ignore.

Very poor sense of self-esteem

This often results in children expressing that they can't do something, or won't like it, as a 'first response' to any suggestion or activity. Children often show a lack of confidence in crossing the 'threshold', which is necessary to engage in an activity. This was described by one parent talking about her daughter as 'she can't help won't'. What she meant by this was that her daughter's condition meant that she *couldn't* help the fact that she *wouldn't* do something at a particular moment. At the same time some children may set themselves unreasonably high standards. Falling short of these standards they set themselves can also then have a negative impact on their self-esteem.

Expressed desire to be equal or better than

Children with PDA often express a desire to be on a par with or better than others, but without seeing it as necessary to put in the effort required. Due to the difficulties they may have in coping with the rigours and demands of practising a task, children with PDA often struggle to improve their skills at a satisfactory pace. This does not mean, however, that they do not wish to excel at some things, so this can bring frustrations. Also they may find it hard to appreciate the efforts others have had to put in to improve their skills.

Desiring friendships but inadvertently sabotaging them

Children with PDA want to have friendships and relationships with other children but often inadvertently sabotage this through their need to be in control, manipulating and mediating or refereeing others' interactions. The child's social interest may be misleading and others may think he has more social understanding and empathy than is in fact the case. The child may blame and victimise other children for things that have gone wrong, even though this is often as a result of his own behaviour. This can include holding grudges over long periods of time and planned retribution for perceived wrongs that have happened earlier.

Ambivalence about success and enjoyment

There is often an ambivalence about succeeding and enjoying an experience or activity, typified by the child who destroys their work on completion when the teacher compliments it.

Lack of permanence and transfer of learning and experience

This means that there can be very sudden and dramatic setbacks for the child after relatively prolonged periods of settled behaviour and progress. Periods of very positive change in school seem to have been largely brought about by the way that staff have been managing the learning environment in some way. This might include reducing and prioritising the demands made, altering the timetable and the way people relate to the child. If these external features revert to how they were, then the child is set back again. It is far harder to bring about long-lasting change within the child himself.

Very poor emotional regulation

This means the child is prone to mood swings and phases that can be either short-lived (minutes or hours) or last for longer periods of time (weeks or months). The child's level of tolerance is very much mood-related and there can be what are best seen as 'can't help it days' when it is unproductive to pursue demands. There is often a sense of the child being emotionally exhausted from 'always being on the watch' for the next demand. This can also result in exhaustion on the part of supporting adults, who feel they are also always on the watch for potential flashpoints. One teacher, writing in a report for an annual review described this:

James has an energetic, extrovert, engaging and mature character. He can also be impulsive, inappropriate, unresponsive and explosive. These extremes of behaviour can make time spent with him exciting and fun, or, exhausting and exasperating. No doubt this must also be the case for James, which must be a rollercoaster ride for him too.

Variability in behaviour

Mood swings or phases mean that the child's behaviour may come across as very variable and inconsistent, which in turn makes them very unpredictable. Both staff and parents frequently describe a sense of 'walking on eggshells' and of being 'lulled in to a false sense of security' (following a relatively calm and tolerant period of behaviour).

Extensive involvement in fantasy and role play

This may happen in a way that cuts off the child and leads to them feeling that they have features of those they mimic or identify with. This can be problematic (e.g. a feeling of omnipotence when identifying with cartoon characters or superheroes).

NEXT STEPS – TOWARDS A FURTHER UNDERSTANDING

The descriptions of the distinctive profile of Pathological Demand Avoidance syndrome are resonating with an increasing number of parents and professionals who recognise how it makes sense of children that were previously difficult to understand within conventional diagnostic concepts. This has contributed to emerging insights into the different emphasis that is needed for interventions with such children to be more effective. These will be explored in the following chapters. In correspondence parents have made comments such as these.

Understanding PDA has helped us to adapt our own thinking to make small concessions which make all the difference to our son.

The diagnosis has helped me understand the reasons behind behaviour hence I now deal with my son in a different way. I avoid direct demands and give him winding down time during the day to help him relax.

Firstly, can we give a heartfelt 'thank you' to all involved with Molly's assessment; we are already experiencing a better home life, even before implementing any specific strategies. It seems that simply by having a better understanding of Molly's difficulties, there is a tangible drop in tension surrounding our interactions.

It is apparent that other research studies and clinical practitioners are identifying the need to define and describe the various sub-groups that may lie within the broad categories of pervasive developmental disorder or autism spectrum disorders. The time now seems right to work collaboratively to further our understanding of PDA and the best ways to support these children, their families and those making educational provision.

Chapter 2

POSITIVE EVERYDAY STRATEGIES

INTRODUCTION

Over recent years those involved in leading and managing services for children with special educational needs have been talking about what they see as a growing number of children with increasingly complex needs. Recently Professor Barry Carpenter (2010) has been writing a series of 'think-pieces for special education' as part of a research project for the Specialist Schools and Academies Trust (an independent, not-for-profit membership organisation dedicated to raising levels of achievement in secondary education). This project has focused on children with complex difficulties and disabilities. He points out that ASD gives rise to severe, profound and complex learning difficulties in some children, often compounded around adolescence as mental health needs may emerge. The article goes on to suggest that there is an 'ever-increasing group of children with complex needs who do not fit the current range of learning environments, curriculum models or teaching and learning approaches and are challenging our most skilled teachers' (think piece 2, p.4).

In the case of those children with PDA, in addition to the research and clinical experience that led on to the production of a detailed clinical description, Newson and colleagues developed some initial guidelines setting out the key implications for education and management of children with this profile (Newson 1998). These continue to be developed collaboratively by other staff from the Elizabeth Newson Centre and

Sutherland House School. They have also been influenced by discussions with parents and through debate with other professionals in the course of outreach consultation and seminars or conferences. The initial driving force underlying this process was the realisation that many of the generally accepted strategies that were advocated for children with autism and Asperger's syndrome were not proving so successful for children with PDA: a different emphasis was required.

When involved with children with PDA it is important to try to strike a balance between providing sufficient predictability to create a sense of security on the one hand, while using novelty and spontaneity to achieve co-operation and engagement on the other.

The following extract is typical of many of the reports that are received by the centre, as part of the process of gathering information to support an assessment. This is from a teacher's description of Jack, a six-year-old with an earlier diagnosis of autism:

No strategy works for long and unlike the other autistic children it is better if we keep changing the routine all the time with Jack. We found the more routine there is the worse he is… you need to catch him unawares. We have tried using behavioural approaches with him but these have not worked. He doesn't seem to understand rewards… do this and then you can have that… he will snatch the reward and then not do the task. He has his set agenda and he is always in control of the situation.

Jack's teacher, working in a special school, highlights some of the key differences in emphasis that are required. The use of structure, routine and behavioural principles of reward, that are usually successful for children with autism or Asperger's syndrome, are less likely to be so effective for children with PDA.

This picture is echoed in comments that parents make:

Getting Duncan to do anything he doesn't want to do is extremely difficult. He will refuse point blank to co-operate and we find that the strategies that you would normally apply with a child don't work with him. He is only motivated by rewards in the short term and although he initially wants the reward, the desire for it is not enough to motivate him to work for it. He isn't bothered by sanctions and will often pre-empt you by saying, 'I don't care, take all my Pokémon things away' or 'Here, throw my Game Boy in the bin'. He rarely makes connections between his actions and consequences, and we find that he shows little remorse when he has harmed someone, but has exaggerated expectations of justice when someone has hurt or upset him.

This is not to suggest that there is simply one set of guidelines that can be applied to children with autism and another that works for children with PDA. It is more a question of the emphasis and prominence that needs to given to particular methods and teaching styles. Ultimately any strategies need to be tailored for the individual child as part of a process of drawing up a programme of personalised learning.

The first part of this chapter focuses on issues and approaches of *education and management* used within school settings, outlining some of the adaptations that are necessary for children with PDA. It starts by discussing the *expectations* of the child *and how to prioritise* the *demands* that we make. This leads on to describing *teaching style*, *strategies* and aspects of *classroom management*. Wider issues of *staff support and whole-school organisation* are referred to but are discussed more fully in Chapter 4. The principles outlined are also applicable to the home, or indeed other situations. Specific issues in *adapting the strategies at home* will be briefly addressed in a later section and in detail in Chapter 3.

EDUCATION AND MANAGEMENT OF CHILDREN WITH PDA

Children with PDA may be provided for in the full range of educational placements that are available. Any particular school will, though, find that they have to make adaptations of one sort or another to meet the precise needs of an individual child with this profile of development and learning.

In broad terms the general aims for any school in attempting to meet the needs of a child with PDA can be summarised as:

- enabling access to learning (both in terms of the curriculum and socially)

- managing the child's anxiety and subsequent behaviour

- supporting positive relationships with his peers

- maintaining an effective team of adults who can support the child and his family.

The remaining sections of this chapter consider how to address the first two of these issues, while supporting relationships with peers and maintaining a staff team are discussed in Chapter 4.

EXPECTATIONS, PRIORITIES AND GROUND RULES

The first thing that any adult must remember when dealing with a child with PDA is that every interaction, or exchange, is a *transactional* (or two-way) *process*. It isn't enough for a teacher to look at the child's behaviour and profile without first considering their own contribution to the situation. It may be a bit of a cliché, but if the adult isn't part of the solution they will become part of the problem.

At the heart of this process is the adults' understanding of PDA, how this affects a particular child and their own ideas about why he might be behaving in certain ways. This is why a distinctive diagnosis is so important. This is not because it gives the child a 'label' but because it acts as a 'signpost' and helps give those adults dealing with the child a framework that they can use to understand the child's behaviour. The way in which we understand his behaviour and the beliefs that we hold about it, inevitably affect our attitudes both towards the child and his behaviour. This, in turn, determines how we approach him (proactively) and respond (reactively) to the way in which he behaves.

Let's take as our starting point the position referred to in the first chapter, and initially articulated by a parent, that the child *'can't help won't'*. If we hold this view we understand that the child's PDA (an anxiety-driven need to be in control and avoid other people's demands and expectations) means that he can't help the fact that he won't do it, on this occasion. This doesn't mean that we simply give up, or give in to, a particular situation. We do, though, understand that the child's anxiety means that he *can't* do it at this time. That means that it is our responsibility as the adult to try to think of ways in which we can help him be less anxious and more tolerant so that he is enabled to do whatever it is that we expect. If, on the other hand, we see the child's avoidance or refusal as being wilful and deliberate (i.e. we simply think that he *won't* do it), it leads us down a path that encourages us to prove that our will is stronger and that, as the adult involved, it is our right and responsibility to impose our choice or decision on the child.

Many parents of children with PDA have found Ross Greene's description of the 'explosive child' very helpful and there are many useful parallels in his book (Greene 2005). One of Greene's guiding ideas is that 'children do well if they *can*' and that explosive children are developmentally delayed in their capacity to be flexible and to tolerate frustration. With these children he counsels against taking the alternative view that 'children do well if they *want to*' and the consequent belief that all parents and others need to do is be firmer, more effective disciplinarians and use conventional behaviour management programmes based on rewards and sanctions. He points out that some children benefit enormously from these sorts of programmes; but for the children he is writing about they often increase the frequency and intensity of the child's explosions and make adults' interactions with their child worse. He goes on to say that being inflexible yourself (e.g. simply demanding and insisting without understanding the child's point of view or being able to compromise) doesn't help the child become more flexible.

This resonates very strongly with our experiences of living and working with children who have PDA. The child's difficulty with co-operation or lack of tolerance isn't something that he can simply overcome by an act of will or by 'trying harder'. As Elizabeth Newson (1988, p.4) recognised in the first handling guidelines for children with PDA:

> There is a real coping problem here which has to be recognised; **the problem is an incapacity** rather than naughtiness. The child literally does not know what other children know by nature about how to behave, and is deeply confused; 'being told' cannot solve the problem, and nor can sanctions.

It must be recognised that for some people reaching this starting point in their understanding is more difficult than for others. The interpretation that people have of the sorts of behaviour that we have described is deeply influenced by their own temperament, attitudes and beliefs. These are much harder to influence than their understanding and skills. In a school situation the staff team may need to work hard to support and develop positive attitudes and may need to allocate certain roles or functions to members of the team who have different strengths. Decisions about who takes on particular roles need to be made on the basis of individual team members' skills and attributes, rather than their position in the school. This requires a degree of flexibility at an organisational level that some schools find easier than others. Time may also need to be spent in finding ways of matching up staff who are a 'best fit' with the child and the style of approach advocated. Sometimes it might need to be recognised and accepted that for certain staff such a match is not in their or the child's best interests.

In an annual review report his teacher described how 'Duncan shows clear preferences for certain staff members and responds well to these people. It has been crucial to build on these positive relationships as they are fundamental to helping him co-operate, negotiate, stay calm and learn. It has been important to try to widen the number of adults he is comfortable with so that the team supporting him can achieve a balance of making him feel secure whilst sharing the load of working so intensely with him. It is worth noting that features these members of staff have in common are a creative, imaginative way of presenting tasks, a non-directive approach and an ability to move on from any difficult incidents without judgment.'

Expectations and ground rules

At the heart of the process of trying to enable a pupil with PDA to have access to learning opportunities is the question of how much to insist that he conforms to the typical expectations within school. The same is true for parents bringing up their child at home. Finding the answer to this question is never straightforward. Compromise, prioritising what is important, flexibility and negotiation should, though, be at the core.

Some examples of Andrew's behaviour and development were given in the first chapter. The following extract comes from the report written by the centre, following his assessment, which illustrates some of the predicaments that are common for many schools. At the time Andrew was in his local mainstream school.

Notes that had been prepared for a recent review at school identified a number of dilemmas in considering Andrew's provision, which included the following.

- Should we insist?

- How much choice can he exercise?

- Should he work to his own curriculum?

These are all questions of balance and are at the heart of planning a programme for a child like Andrew. Decisions need, at one level, to be made day by day according to his mood and tolerance, which can be very variable, both over the short term and longer periods of time. The level of challenging behaviour that Andrew demonstrates in school is, clearly, likely to be reduced if he is able to follow his interests through a differentiated curriculum, exercise his own choice and when demands on him aren't too great. At the same time, the long-term consequence of this is that it reinforces his desire to be in control and does not contribute to his inclusion. One of the most important issues is staff being clear and in agreement about what are priorities in terms of behaviour and expectations and what can be tolerated at a particular time. There are likely to be periods when Andrew feels more relaxed, trusting in the relationships he has with staff and more tolerant of what other people want of him. At these times more can be expected in the way of conformity and encouragement to accept other people's expectations. There will be other periods when the opposite is true and it will be necessary for him to be put under less pressure.

It is also important for all staff within the school to have as good an understanding of Andrew's needs as possible. It is easy to interpret a PDA child's avoidant behaviour as being deliberately wilful and provocative, especially when they have the ability that Andrew does.

Inevitably much of the above is of a general nature and the details need to be negotiated and agreed within school.

This example raises some key points about the school's immediate management of Andrew: the need to *choose priorities*, day-to-day *adjustment of demands according to variation in his tolerance* and the need for planning to be informed by discussion and continual monitoring.

Choosing priorities

While it is, of course, important to have high expectations of children, the school day and classroom environment is full of demands. Typically developing children can usually accommodate these easily but they provoke high levels of anxiety for the majority of children with PDA. It can be tempting to think that all children need to conform to the same rules and expectations, but real inclusion is about appropriate differentiation, personalisation and having the flexibility to adapt to individual needs. If PDA is understood as an anxiety-driven need to be in control and avoid other people's demands and expectations, it is essential to think about which particular situations are provoking high levels of anxiety for the child at this particular point in time. Once these have been identified, the next stage is asking ourselves openly and honestly 'How important is this at the moment?'. Both within Sutherland House, and as part of outside consultation, some sort of checklist is used and can be a useful way of structuring these decisions and helping to choose priorities.

Neil (aged 10) had recently started a new school following an exclusion from his previous school followed by several months at home. There were some tensions around getting him to attend school on a daily basis and he had particular issues regarding being amongst the hustle and bustle of the other pupils.

It was an immediate priority to keep him sufficiently relaxed and confident about coming to school, and lots of accommodations were made around this point. For example, he came to school by taxi, though often had difficulty getting from the taxi into school. While he settled in, the taxi drove onto the school playground 20 minutes after the other children had gone into school. Neil could then get out of the taxi and make his way into school in his own time. On delicate days, this meant that he was at least safely on school grounds so that the taxi was free to leave even if it took some careful negotiating to get from the playground into the classroom.

Table 2.1 Priority rating chart (school)

Prioritising behaviour – How important is it that this pupil…?	Priority rating	Comments
sits on a chair during classroom teaching sessions	3	*More important to stay in designated area of class to minimise disruption to others.*
keeps shoes on inside school	3	*Having shoes on to go outdoors will be a requirement, but doesn't have to join in playtime.*
attends assembly	3	*Not important – in fact can we use this time for personal tutorials? Additional PHSE work?*
does not damage property	1	*Non-negotiable – he will be prevented from doing this.*
uses pupil toilets at school	3	*More important that he uses a toilet at school – will nominate particular toilet for his use.*
does not hurt other people (adults or children)	1	*Non-negotiable – he will be prevented from doing this.*
completes homework tasks	3	*Important to reduce pressure at home – keep option open for home/school 'project work'.*
lines up with class group	3	*More important to walk round school calmly – maybe develop 'monitor' role instead of lining up?*
does not hurt himself	1	*Non-negotiable – he will be prevented from doing this.*
answers teacher when register called	3	*Not worth seeing through – could develop alternative way of 'signing in'?*
changes into PE kit	3	*For safety reasons may need to change or remove shoes – PE kit available in case chosen.*
joins in class-based group activities	2	*Priority times for joining peer group are for social opportunities not teaching.*
records all his work in his own handwriting	3	*Can dictate, draw, use ICT, digital photos, Dictaphone.*
feels positive about being in school and develops emotional well-being	1	*High priority.*
Any other category you feel is a priority for your child/your setting which is missing from this list? Goes home feeling as calm and settled as possible	1	*Will have opportunity for games/chat/ relaxation from 3 – 3.30 each day.*

Priority rating:
1 = high priority in all circumstances
2 = highly desirable but not essential
3 = low priority – we need to work around this another way

At an after school meeting, classroom staff used the checklist in Table 2.1 to shape a discussion of priorities for him which could then be used as a shared framework and could then inform any specific behaviour plans needed to support the priority ratings.

Staff attending the meeting included, class teacher, teaching assistant, SENCO, speech and language therapist, and head teacher. After the meeting, information was fed back and discussed with parents.

For some children, who may present in quite extreme ways, initially this list can be very short indeed.

Due to Duncan's very negative reactions to school, following successive failed placements it was crucial for him to have a positive introduction and transition. A decision was made, in consultation with his family to have only three immovable ground rules in the early days. These were: no hurting yourself, no hurting other people and no damaging property. His timetable was highly individualised with very little expectation to join group sessions at structured teaching times, and all work was to be done through games and projects.

A similar list can be used in a family discussion at home and an example can be found in Chapter 3, p.81. As well as helping focus on priorities this enables everyone concerned to recognise that there can be different views and perspectives about what is important.

It is crucial, though, to reach a consensus and agreement about just what those priorities are. Another aim within this process is to try and remove some of the situations that cause the child anxiety and have the potential to cause conflict. It gives 'permission', for the moment at least, to make a positive decision to 'let some things go'. That in turn means that adults can preserve their attention for what has been agreed as most important.

Adjusting demands according to level of tolerance

Of course, these chosen priorities need to be monitored and kept under review as part of the pupil's individual plan. It is hoped that, as the child gradually becomes more trusting and confident in school, expectations can be progressively increased, but these are likely to need to be adapted on a day-to-day basis according to the child's level of mood and tolerance. The variation in a child's mood and tolerance has been described several times. It is best to see this in terms of him having a particular 'threshold' in relation to his capacity for tolerating demands. This threshold is determined by the level of anxiety that he feels at any given point in time. His level of anxiety can, in turn, be influenced by a multitude of factors, which include short-term influences (e.g. how well he slept the night before, whether a trusted member of staff is present or absent, what another child said to him on his way across the playground, etc.) or longer-term ones (e.g. he is in a settled phase with trusting relationships, he has just moved up from primary school, etc.). When things are going well and his anxiety is low, this threshold is higher and he can be more accepting of demands and requests. When it is more difficult, his anxiety is raised and his threshold is low. At these times he is less tolerant, feels the need to be more controlling and is easily 'tipped over the edge'. Figure 2.1 is an attempt to represent what is perhaps the key challenge in teaching and managing a child with PDA, getting the balance between adult expectation and the child's capacity to cope. It shows two dials, one of which illustrates the level of the child's threshold or tolerance, the other represents the extent of demand that he experiences. At times, *when his threshold is high* it is possible to raise expectations, increase demands and attempt to be more directive. *When his threshold is low* the dial representing the level of demand needs to be adjusted to the left, reducing the pressure he feels. The teacher, or parent, has to try and keep the two dials in synchrony for as much time as possible. The frequency with which these dials need adjusting varies from child to child and will change over time. There will be spells when they need almost constant fine-tuning to try and keep things on as even a keel as possible. In other situations there might be quite long settled spells when much less adjustment is needed. While long settled spells are, of course, encouraging for everybody, it is important to guard against complacency. So many teachers and parents report to us how good spells can be punctuated by a sudden 'blip' and describe how they had 'let slide some of the things we had been doing that had enabled him to become more tolerant'.

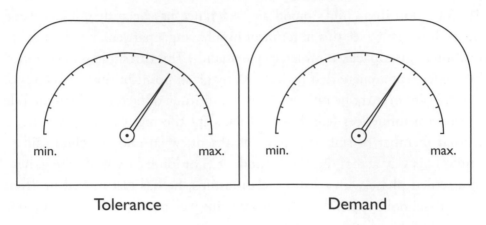

Tolerance   Demand

Figure 2.1 Synchronising adult expectation and the child's tolerance

This process of choosing priorities and adjusting expectations doesn't, as was said earlier, mean that we simply give up, or give in to, a particular situation. The next section looks at some of the ways in which we can help him become less anxious and more tolerant, so that he is enabled to do more of those things that are expected of him. There will, of course, be times for everyone involved with a child with PDA that they will be in a position where it is necessary to *maintain ground rules*. It is hoped that by adopting the attitudes outlined and employing some of the flexible and creative strategies we go on to describe, the frequency that an impasse occurs is kept to a minimum. There may, though, be occasions when this point is reached, the child's anxiety escalates and results in a 'meltdown' that needs to be managed.

Managing meltdowns

There are times when children with PDA may use aggression as way of trying to avoid demands, or will lash out at someone in anger. This section isn't about these sorts of occurrences. It is about the sort of explosive panic attack that is often described as a 'meltdown'. This is a term that Lipsky and Richards (2009), in their book *Managing Meltdowns* describing calming techniques for people with autism, define as a 'catastrophic reaction'. The reason for such a reaction is, of course, specific to each individual child and particular situation. It is though almost certainly underpinned by the child's anxiety reaching a point that the pressure he feels under becomes intolerable and he sees no 'way out'.

Meltdowns can have an alarming intensity and may, literally, go on for hours. The child may scream, rage, kick, hit, bite and throw objects. Clearly instances such as these are distressing for the child, those trying to deal with the outburst and anyone who witnesses it. The first objective must therefore be to keep the dials in synchrony and avoid episodes occurring, or at least reduce them to a minimum. As described above, it is important to choose priorities carefully, some confrontations may need to be 'seen through' because a boundary has been crossed that we have determined is not negotiable. Some meltdowns are unavoidable and it should not be seen as a failure if one occurs. At the same time, though, it is important to reflect back on a situation after it has occurred to see what can be learnt from it.

Sometimes there will be signs indicating that an explosion is a potential and it might be possible to avoid the situation by distracting, adjusting the demand or compromising in some way. At other times there may be no obvious precipitating factors. Once a meltdown is truly underway, though, the child will be beyond reason, and using complicated language and negotiation at this stage is likely to be counter-productive. Indeed reducing any further demand at this point and keeping language and eye-contact to a minimum is likely to be much more effective. Some children will be helped by calm reassurance and affirmation, where the child's emotion is recognised (e.g. 'I know that you are upset'). Ensuring that the child and those around him are as safe as possible has to be the main consideration. In a classroom situation this may mean moving other children away or guiding the child to a designated safe area (an example of this is given in the section on environment later in this chapter).

After the episode has run its course, a time for calming and recovery is necessary. Sometimes children with PDA seem to have some sense of realisation that they have, in a way, crossed a line and need nurturing to regain their composure. At other times they can calm much more quickly, almost as though the event had never occurred. It may be harder for the adult, particularly, a parent, to draw a line under the episode. In schools the staff team need to be aware of how each individual may be affected and provide an opportunity for debriefing and support (more detail of this will be given in the section on staff support in Chapter 4, p.123).

Seeing a meltdown through can have some positive aspects and can, in some ways, reinforce a relationship if handled well. This is likely to involve the adult supporting the child through the episode positively and not being judgemental afterwards. Accepting the child and being non-judgemental, though, doesn't meant that nothing can be learnt from the episode. All staff in schools need to reflect on their practice and might ask themselves questions such as those in the list below. A similar process might also be helpful for parents and family members.

- Should I stand by the boundaries set? If not, why not? Are they realistic? Are they important enough to be non-negotiable?

- Did I overreact? If so, why? Can I get more advice/support from?

- What did I do well? Can I use some of these successful strategies again in the future?

- If I ask in the right way, will the child be able to tell me more about why that went particularly well/badly for him?

- Did I get the balance right between encouragement and directness?

- Are there any other strategies I wish I'd tried?

Discussing the meltdown with the child or young person after the event can also be extremely valuable if done sensitively and in the context of a trusting relationship. This does need to be done with caution, and for some children being asked to re-live the event at the wrong time, or in the wrong way, can make matters worse. The child can be made to feel that the discussion is largely about retribution and can bring the anger back to the fore. The sort of mentoring and tutorial discussions that are detailed in Chapter 5 on promoting emotional well-being are an ideal forum for many children. It enables both parties to look back on situations, talk about what worked well and what didn't, and plan for future alternative strategies in a proactive way. This might include helping children identify the situations that can cause extreme anxiety, recognise the warning signs that they are building up to an explosion and think of ways that they might be able to defuse the situation in some way.

TEACHING STYLE AND STRATEGIES AND CLASSROOM MANAGEMENT

Relationships and personal style

The quality of relationship(s) between the adult and child is fundamental. A key-worker system is usually the most effective in the early stages when a child is new to the school or setting. The key-worker can build up an intimate knowledge of the child and know when to pursue an objective and when to reduce pressure, making continual adjustments as needed. A successful relationship works both ways. As children build up and accumulate trust in the individual worker, they become more confident in their ability to adapt accordingly and trust that this adult will ease them through situations that they find too confrontational or overwhelming.

A teacher described this in her report about a child in her class. 'As we have come to know Luke better, he has increasingly begun to trust us and we have been able to use this relationship to offer time to talk him through difficult moments. This has been invaluable not only in preventing some incidents but also in helping him through incidents if one does become unavoidable.'

When a child starts at a new school the thoroughness of the transition can vary considerably. In some cases it will be part of a gradual exchange of information with parents and other professionals, a series of preliminary visits and a measured hand-over. This depends on a whole range of factors such as the age of the child, the prominence of their needs, whether or not they have been in previous placement, etc. It is usually best to take time to 'sit back' and observe at first, and to place few demands while the relationship develops. In practice a single relationship of this sort can cause organisational problems for a school, put undue pressure on the adult concerned and lead to dependency on the part of the child. In the initial stages it may be the quickest and most effective way of building a relationship. As time progresses, though, it is best if this role can be shared among a small group.

AVOID BEING DIRECTIVE

The style needs to be highly individualised *but less directive* and more intuitive than would ordinarily be the case with children with autism. Invitations or suggestions, such as 'I wonder how we might?' or 'I can't quite see how to do...' are often more effective than more direct instructions such as 'Now let's get on with...'. Adults need to empower the child by giving more choices and where possible allow him to have a feeling of being in control.

At first Duncan became anxious and unco-operative when expected to individually complete a piece of curriculum work presented to him within classroom sessions, refusing verbally or leaving the room. As a way of reducing the pressure that he felt, the teacher decided to leave out three alternative activities which were all related to the curriculum work. Duncan was given total choice of which he wanted to do.

Strategies that were effective in helping Sarah to co-operate were: using role play, humour, being less directive, pretending you didn't know something and choosing carefully when to ignore minor negative behaviours.

Humour is one of the most important parts of Jack's interaction at school, with both peers and staff. He has most trust and respect for those who can relate to and share his sense of humour. It is important for Jack to see that adults genuinely enjoy his company. In addition, enjoying and indulging in his sense of fun in some areas means it is easier to raise expectations of him to co-operate in others.

KEEP CALM

Adults need to *keep calm and level in their own emotions* in the face of challenging or disruptive behaviour and situations that they may find frustrating. The child with PDA is adept at reading these reactions (even if he doesn't fully empathise with the emotions behind them) and may gain a certain satisfaction from the excitement that this behaviour can bring about. It is important not to take things personally, even if some of the child's behaviour seems to be directed at specific people.

Hannah went through a period where she would occupy the teacher's chair at the front of the class as the pupils were gathered for a group instruction. Hannah would then refuse to vacate the chair, and insistence would lead to noisy and disruptive behaviour, often escalating to a point where other staff needed to become involved and physical intervention was required. After discussion the teacher decided to ignore this behaviour and carry on addressing the group. She asked the rest of the class to move to the back of the room, where there was some soft seating. Hannah would then dash over to secure a soft chair and after a few moments the class were able to return to their usual positions.

BE FLEXIBLE

It is crucial to be *flexible and adaptable* and it is likely that strategies will need to be changed much more frequently than would be the case for a child with autism. What works one day, may not work the next, but it may be worth coming back to in the future. This requires stamina and ingenuity on the part of staff if a sense of purpose and direction is still to be maintained and can require on the spot decision-making. What is important is for the adults to ask themselves how they can help the child to succeed in a given situation. When resistance and avoidance are encountered it is helpful to think about ways in which the demand can be modified or adapted in some way, reaching a compromise rather than allowing the situation to escalate into a confrontation. The child may not be able to achieve what was expected at that very moment but may, though, begin to make a series of achievements towards this end as trust and confidence build.

During a PE lesson where the use of apparatus was required Adam started to insist that he couldn't participate because 'my legs don't work'. He was new to the class and staff were starting to recognise that he would frequently try to avoid activities using similar excuses. They had already found themselves getting into protracted negotiations with him over other issues. On this occasion they decided not to get drawn in to such discussion and joined in with him to make it a game to see which pieces of equipment they could get across only using their arms.

Structured teaching and visual support

The use of structured teaching methods (e.g. providing a strong sense of routine with clearly defined expectations) and visual support (such as the use of symbols to support understanding of language, visual timetables, written messages, mind maps and cartoon drawings to aid social understanding, etc.) have become an integral part of good practice in the education of children with autism. It is not within the realm of this book to give a detailed description of this approach to teaching, and it is well described in a whole range of publications. Those who are less familiar with such methodology will find a comprehensive and useful overview in the Autism Education Trust publication *Tools for Teachers: Practical Strategies for Classroom Success* (2010). Some of these principles and resources can be useful for many children with PDA, depending on their stage of development and their own unique learning profile. They are, though, not as universally helpful as is the case with other children on the autism spectrum. Many children with PDA will exploit routine and predictability. Jack's teacher, in the report that was quoted at the start of the chapter, found that he was better when they 'changed the routine all the time'. While this might seem rather extreme those working with children with PDA find that *novelty and variety is often effective*. This might include variety in the pace of presentation and personal style, which can often intrigue the child. Creating a sense of mystery and suspense can be also helpful; many teachers describe the value of 'pulling rabbits out of the hat'. This can feel counter-intuitive for those experienced in working with children with autism who are used to being very clear in the way they explain, for example, a sequence of tasks that they are about to expect of a child.

Some of the resources commonly used to provide visual support for children with autism can also be extremely useful for children with PDA, but perhaps for rather different reasons. It can have the effect of de-personalising the request or instruction (see below). Using written lists of activities or suggestions can also become a useful basis for negotiation between an adult and child. The following extract is taken from another observational report of a child seen for assessment at the centre. Drawing up the list together gave him a greater sense of control in the process of agreeing activities to be completed, but within this he would still decline certain suggestions and employ delaying tactics. This meant that the psychologist needed to make adaptations as she went on, such as giving activities names that were more 'acceptable' or creating a challenge by suggesting a time limit.

By far the most successful strategy was to draw up a list of activities and games which Kayleigh and Madoc took turns to choose. This provided a visual structure for the afternoon, and a reminder for Madoc to refer to. Although he declined her request to write his choices, and again moved away from her by climbing the climbing frame, he suggested his choices verbally. Kayleigh was able to include tasks within these, re-naming them in ways which would appeal to Madoc; for example, 'drawing' and 'story telling'.

In the later session, Kayleigh again used the list to provide a reference. They chose four activities and worked through each one; to build an army from the Make a World set, to draw pictures, to play shops, and to play Pictionary. Madoc followed the list, although often delayed and distracted Kayleigh. For example, he spent approximately 15 minutes preparing his Make a World army for battle, but did not respond to Kayleigh's requests to begin their fight. Instead, he delayed by listing all the weapons his army had, and frequently checked for more pieces. Again, Kayleigh gave Madoc a time limit, and this helped to encourage him to finish preparing, and begin playing.

Building on a child's strengths and interests

This is an important element of drawing up a tailor-made programme and would be advocated for all children on the autism spectrum, however unusual these may at times seem. Strong interest or fascinations can provide a medium for presenting all sorts of learning opportunities.

SPECIAL INTERESTS AS REWARDS

The use of special interests as rewards (e.g. allowing a child access to a period of time looking at a book about a favourite topic or character after he has completed activities set by an adult) would also be a commonly accepted strategy for children with other ASDs.

Duncan was highly resistant to completing any task that he perceived as 'set school work'. He particularly avoided anything involving writing or working with a group of peers. However, he enjoyed finding out about subjects in which he had a current interest and, once engaged, showed an inquisitive capacity to learn. He became interested in the *Horrid History* television programmes, especially in the Romans, and liked to find out gruesome facts about how they lived, what they ate, their standards of hygiene and how they died.

We decided to capitalise on this interest, in a style which would suit him.

By letting him lead the topic choice, and by tactfully facilitating his research or recording, we were able to work for half a term on the back of the Romans. He was willing to cook some Roman recipes in order to dare staff to taste them; he was interested in finding out how everyone in Pompeii died, which led him to complete some science investigations related to volcanoes; he was motivated to practise telling the time in order to check if his sundial was accurate. Throughout these activities there was an attitude of doing things for the sake of fun or for interest rather than emphasising the learning element. The role of staff was to ease his path through these investigations, taking care often to do a greater share of the background work, guiding him towards success in a sensitively paced manner and respecting his superior knowledge as he gathered new information.

Star charts and similar behavioural strategies can have their place but are less consistently successful for children with PDA and require rather more caution in the way that they are used. Some children even find accepting praise difficult and will refute the suggestion that they have done something well or even destroy the work that has been complimented. At these times it as though the praise or reward signifies for the child not that he has been successful but that he has complied. Some children with greater self-awareness will even talk about not wanting to be 'tricked' by the adult. Sometimes introducing 'surprise' rewards or perks can be effective ways of avoiding a child having the pressure of working towards a specific and pre-determined goal but still reward them for their achievements.

Edwin now responds quite positively to rewards when he has done something noteworthy, therefore we were encouraged when a new reward system was introduced to the class at the start of term. Tokens were awarded, for example, for good work, acts of kindness, etc. Although Edwin enjoys collecting tokens and redeeming them for prizes, he finds the whole system very stressful. His low self-esteem make him feel under pressure to get more tokens than other pupils, which of course is not easily achievable. His issues with interpreting social interaction make him sensitive when others are awarded tokens, which he then takes very personally. The difficulties he has with prediction make it hard for him to appreciate what types of acts or behaviour can earn tokens, which makes the system feel unpredictable and outside his control. His anxiety over expectations to conform mean that the system brings additional stress to his school day, rather than the additional encouragement and motivation it is designed to bring.

Although some rewards can be effective with Edwin, it was necessary to reconsider the appropriateness and indeed the fairness of expecting him to be part of the class token system. It has worked better for him to have a separate system of rewards that is not comparable to other children in the class. This is a system which is clearly outlined and personalised; which sometimes, in negotiation, goes on hold for periods of time; which accrues unexpected 'perks' or treats on occasion; which has a flexible way of 'spending' points earned and is in Edwin's control.

USING DRAMA AND ROLE PLAY

Drama and role play make use of the child's interest in imaginative play. Some children can be encouraged to engage in one-to-one work if they are given the role of the teacher, others will engage more readily if a task is presented via a puppet or imaginative character.

Lenny the Lion has been an invaluable character in recent weeks. Heather is able to coach Lenny through completing tasks which she would not feel able to co-operate with on her own. She can be a hard taskmaster towards Lenny and even threatens him with no food if he doesn't do as he's told. Staff who read Heather well have been able to use subtle ways to also explore themes around friendship, kindness, physical boundaries, etc. in conversations through Lenny.

Monitoring and adjusting your use of language

Children with PDA tend to have less difficulty with comprehension of language than other children on the spectrum. However, their capacity to express themselves and divert or distract an adult in an articulate way can also mask their understanding of certain situations. Many children with PDA do seem to take longer to process language than other children, in part due to their anxiety levels, and often their feeling of being 'hurried' by an adult can contribute to difficult behaviour. It can be helpful to wait just a little longer than might at first seem natural before repeating, re-phrasing or following up a request. At times when a child is particularly agitated it is usually better to avoid getting drawn into lengthy explanations and reduce the language used to the minimum. At other times, though, *using quite complex language can be effective* for smoothing over a request or capturing a child's interest. This may go against the commonly accepted use of concise language styles for children with autism. Concise language can come across to the child with PDA as confrontational, while more complex language tends to feel more negotiative and may also intrigue the child. One mother reported how her son would be more likely to follow an instruction like 'Would you do me the honour of putting on your shoes?'.

Getting into the habit of making simple adjustments to the way that language is used is central to adopting the indirect style that can be so effective for children with PDA. Using language that feels like an invitation is being offered, a suggestion being made, a problem shared, or the child's help is needed feels much less pressuring to the child than directive, instructional language. For example, 'I wonder if…', 'I wish I knew someone who could…', 'What do you think about…?'. Sometimes simple creative re-labelling of activities can be helpful.

This may be as simple as re-naming work tasks as 'missions'. For example, 'Today's challenge, should you wish to take on the mission, is, (using only the materials provided) to simulate a jet-propelled vehicle'.

Nicola often finds it easier to respond to work tasks if they are presented as multiple-choice worksheets, quizzes or as true-or-false activities. The additional benefit of her becoming comfortable with this format is that she can also use these systems to communicate when she is becoming distressed since she struggles to access fluent verbal communication at times of increased agitation.

De-personalising demands and requests

It is often not the task itself that the child finds demanding but the fact that it is another person that has made the request, the child's anxiety being fuelled by their fear of not being in control of the agenda. It can often be helpful to think of ways to de-personalise what is being asked by handing over responsibility (e.g. 'I'm sorry but it's in the health and safety policy that everyone has to…') or presenting the request in another way (e.g.

using a symbol sequence strip or written information and not making further comment)

Joseph was keen about using the computer within class but was finding it very hard to accept it when staff told him he would have to finish, even when they gave him a warning or a countdown to try to help him with the transition. His teacher decided to use an electronic timer which played a pre-recorded message, such as a favourite TV theme tune, which indicated 'game over'. Joseph found this much easier to accept than when a member of staff gave him this message directly.

A parent developed a similar sort of strategy to help overcome her six-year-old son's reluctance to get up in the morning (a very commonly reported issue). She was faced each morning with a torrent of excuses, verbal abuse and physical resistance which lasted up to half an hour and was placing great pressure on the whole family. Speaking at a conference in Nottingham a few years ago she described her solution to the problem. 'While out shopping with Daniel I saw an alarm clock that he wanted. So I bought it…this made Daniel feel in control as he had made the request and I said yes. He thought he was in control…little did he know! He was so excited when we got home, we unpacked it and put in the batteries. I placed the clock just out of his reach; he had to get out of bed to turn it off. The following morning at seven o'clock the alarm clock was the one who had to get Daniel out of bed, and it didn't stop until he got up to switch it off. Daniel still groaned but not at me or anyone else, just the clock! That was quite a while ago now and the alarm clock still goes off at seven o'clock and Daniel still gets out of bed to turn it off. A simple but creative solution is usually the answer. Don't ask me if this strategy will still be working this time next year!'

Environment

All practitioners in education settings need to reflect on the environment and consider how it impacts on children's learning; this includes keeping children safe and looking at aspects of the environment that might be promoting or hindering learning. This has become an increasingly important consideration in provision for children across the autism spectrum, influenced by some of the principles of structured teaching and also by an increasing awareness of the sensory differences that children with ASD experience. The documentation on supporting children on the autism spectrum, produced as part of the Inclusion Development Programme, contains a useful description of this (DCSF 2009a). It includes sections on visual support materials, noise levels, visual distractions, lighting, giving the child space and clearly defined areas.

A local autism outreach team, which had some well-established links with both the Elizabeth Newson Centre and Sutherland House School, gave this area a high profile in their work supporting children in mainstream settings. They described how it was important for the child to be accommodated, not 'isolated or engulfed' and that it often reduced pressure for the child to be 'allowed to be on the fringes', which frequently gave opportunities for incidental learning. They also advocated an area within the class designated for that child's use, somewhere they could have their things and use as a bolt hole or 'place of safety'. For children with explosive behaviour, having a den or safe haven can be especially valuable. It gives the child somewhere they can have space and time. It can allow the staff a pause for breath and give the child dignified privacy to compose themselves before they rejoin the group.

Duncan had the use of a room adjacent to the classroom known as 'the den'. He could use this for time away from the noisy environment of the classroom, for time to relax, and for time to discuss what is happening that day or to review what has happened during the day. He also used the den when he became agitated, as a safe place to calm. He started more frequently to take himself to calm in the den at the request of staff if an incident developed, and even requested to do so appropriately himself. He was generally accompanied in the den by members of staff with whom he has closer relationships. He also decorated the den and started to take responsibility for it as his environment. There were occasions when he used the den to avoid a work task. Depending on the circumstances and his mood, the work was either taken with him into the den or it waited in the classroom to be done on his return. It was really important though that he viewed the den as a comfortable area to be used regularly, often just to chat or play, and to make sure that it was a positive environment for him.

EMOTIONAL WELL-BEING AND THE LONGER-TERM VIEW

For the majority of children with PDA the prevailing state of their approach to school and learning is one of anxiety, which for a number of children impacts on their willingness to come to school in the first place (the ultimate avoidance). Unsurprisingly, this anxiety is largely driven by the child's perception of real or potential demands; thereby being faced with failure and not being in control. The strategies described are all aimed at reducing the feeling of pressure that the child senses. More specific techniques, such as teaching relaxation, increasing the amount of physical exercise, etc., can all be valuable.

Most of what has been said so far has focused on strategies to help reduce the child's anxiety, increase their engagement and participation in learning. This has concentrated on adapting and managing their immediate environment in some way. It is also important to consider ways in which we might look beyond these immediate adaptations and foster longer-term personal understanding and awareness, which enables the child better to regulate their own responses and reactions.

The UK curriculum now gives a much higher priority to the concept of 'emotional literacy' for all children. This presents real opportunities for children with complex social and communication differences. An important aspect of raising emotional well-being is to develop a level of self-awareness in young people for them to have realistic expectations of themselves that value them for the person they are. As they mature, this will lead them to make more appropriate choices regarding hobbies, social opportunities, potential employment and a place to live. For children with PDA this may well include developing an understanding of their diagnosis. This needs to be done carefully over time and needs to be highly individualised. It is a complex issue which ought not to be undertaken lightly. For more detail on self-awareness and explaining the diagnosis to young people see Chapter 5.

Earlier we gave an example taken from a report about Andrew, which was used to illustrate the issues of choosing priorities and adjusting demands according to his varying level of tolerance. The following extract from his report discusses the longer-term issue of considering his self-awareness and personal understanding.

In addition to present management issues, consideration needs to be given to proactive and longer-term approaches. As Andrew grows older it will be increasingly appropriate and necessary to encourage him to understand the nature of some of his own emotions, difficulties and the consequences that his behaviour has. In terms of differentiating his curriculum, emphasis needs to be given to personal and social education, and the use of individual 'mentoring' or 'personal tutorial' sessions can be very helpful here. This sort of daily 'special time' can be used to plan and negotiate the day's activities, reflect on what has gone well and not so well and spend time on discussions to do with likes and dislikes, emotional understanding, things we find hard and difficult, etc. Some of the work developed for children with Asperger's syndrome can be usefully adapted here. The social stories approach developed by Carol Gray has a lot of useful ideas in relation to self-awareness (such as 'colouring your emotions'). More recently we have had very positive feedback from staff and parents using *Asperger's... What Does It Mean to Me?* a workbook written by Catherine Faherty (2000). Some of the worksheets and activities in this have been adapted to suit children with PDA and may be useful for Andrew.

ADAPTING THE STRATEGIES TO HOME

While the vast majority of children with PDA show their avoidance both at home and school (i.e. it is pervasive), this isn't always to the same extent at the same point in time. Some children may be going through 'good phases' at home while they are having a 'bad phase' at school, or vice versa. In addition, they may feel better able to co-operate with a given task more easily in one place than another. For example, a child may dress and undress without issues for school swimming sessions, but getting dressed at home is a battle every morning. There are, though, a small group of children who are much more variable across the two settings. They may be much more avoidant and controlling at home than they are at school where they seem to 'slip under the radar'. Alternatively it is the school environment that they find especially challenging and find it easier at home because the environment can be more adaptive and responsive. This is just one of the reasons that it is crucial for schools and parents to work together in an open and supportive partnership.

Most of the strategies described earlier in the chapter have been written from a school perspective, but many of the principles can be adapted to home. Home situations and families' attitudes to bringing up children can vary as much as the way in which schools approach issues on inclusion and behaviour. In general they can afford to be more adaptive and place fewer demands than most schools. At the same there are likely to be all sorts of different pressures resulting from family life and the needs of other family members, which can cause different pressures and make individualisation harder. Also parents don't have the luxury of their responsibility finishing at the end of the school day.

Chapter 3 considers some of the issues and strategies from a parental perspective.

Chapter 3

LIVING WITH PDA

THE IMPACT OF PDA IN THE HOME

There are difficulties and stresses living with any child with additional needs, and PDA is no exception. Of course, the overriding feature of PDA is the inability to deal with simple requests just for the everyday things in life that we all take for granted. It must be remembered that children with PDA experience an anxiety-driven need to avoid demands, and are not simply willful or contrary. The average parents having an average morning with average kids may not realise that to a child with PDA, that 'average' morning is loaded with demands:

'Get up.'
'Get your clothes on.'
'Wash your face.'
'Brush your teeth.'
'Comb your hair.'
'Eat your breakfast.'
'Take your tablets.'
'Find your homework.'
'Get your schoolbag.'
'Fetch your lunchbox'.
'Put your shoes on.'
'Get your coat on.'
'Put that down we have to go.'
'Come on the bus is waiting.'

Imagine if every one of those demands was met with anxiety. Imagine if every time parents asked their child to do one of those things, they were met with a tirade of excuses, delaying tactics, refusals, swearing, spitting, abuse and sometimes violence. This has to be juggled with all the other things that must be done in the morning, like going to work and getting other children ready. There may be the added pressure of being a single parent. Imagine the impact that has on the parents, the siblings and the relationships within that family. It is demoralising, frustrating and can make any sane person question their parenting skills. It is surprising that the child even gets out of the house. Well, sometimes he doesn't.

Welcome to the household with a child who has PDA.

Although this is an example of a typical morning, it is still very difficult to explain to someone what living with a child with this condition is like. Often as time goes on, parents become so used to the compensations and the adjustments which they have developed that they forget how differently ordinary families live.

Demands and anxiety

As described in Chapter 2, the child with PDA displays an anxiety-driven need to be in control and avoid other people's demands and expectations. This, in turn, can lead to negative behaviours. Occasionally, sanctions can be helpful, but generally they are not and punishments are often ineffective. A child with PDA often knows what people should and shouldn't do – they just find it very difficult to apply that to themselves! By the time parents read this book, many will have already tried traditional parenting techniques. The latter, such as those seen in popular parenting television programmes, typically feature a parenting expert who observes and makes recommendations. These suggestions usually involve being very directive with children, and using 'time out' techniques. Parents may have tried these techniques over and over and will have reached the conclusion that their child just doesn't seem to respond to those – in fact, for the child with PDA, often their behaviour worsens. This is because, as the demand increases so does the need to resist it.

Reducing anxiety is paramount. What causes that anxiety will of course vary with each child's tolerance and on what sort of day he's having.

We already know that the demands themselves cause anxiety in these individuals. Often there are other factors associated with those demands too, like a sensory problem (e.g. too loud or too scratchy) or a change to what the child had perceived might happen. Getting to know your child and what makes them anxious is a huge step to second guessing what will cause them difficulties. If you know what can cause them anxiety you can take steps to remove or adjust those things and reassure the child. As they mature, they can develop ways in which they can solve those problems more independently in the future.

Let us assume, for example, that getting a child to put his clothes on causes anxiety. First it may cause anxiety because it is a demand, and second because the child may be worried that the clothes are itchy or feel scratchy. The latter may also be an avoidance tactic, but removing any anxiety associated with a demand is helpful. If he knows he can wear a favourite T-shirt that feels very soft he may be more inclined to agree with the demand than if it's a new T-shirt. Even if some anxiety about complying remains, the chances of resisting have at least reduced.

Of course not every day will be the same. The child's tolerance and anxiety will vary some days more than others, and managing this effectively will depend on how easy it is for families to keep the degree of demand synchronised with the degree of tolerance. The analogy of the dials is a useful one (see Figure 2.1 on p.52). A child may one day be having a 'good day' and he may manage to contend with some demands, but if he is having a 'not-so-good day', every demand may be a cause of major anxiety, and anxiety in these children often translates into frustration, avoidance or anger. On the other hand, some children can have extended spells of tolerance, which may even last several weeks at a time. When this happens, families are often lulled into a false sense of security, since their child appears in most ways to be coping with life and hasn't had an outburst for a while. This can have the effect of adults 'forgetting' the impact of using strategies which have helped their child to be less anxious and therefore more co-operative. Over time, this erosion of a different style of managing and parenting can lead towards new episodes of difficult behaviour.

Sometimes this coincides with people telling parents there is nothing wrong with their child, so the parents, wishing their child to be 'normal' also think that there is nothing wrong. The difficulty with this situation is that it can lead to a belief that the child's issues must just be down to poor parenting and that employing the 'conventional' parenting techniques, which have been used successfully for all their other children, will offer a solution. When their child switches from the polite, calm child of yesterday into a raving, biting, scratching 'Mr Hyde' once again, the parents sink, devastated, into desperation, bewildered by their child's behaviour and confused about where to turn next.

Mood swings, obsessions and role play

One of the difficult aspects of PDA is the child's seeming ability to switch from one mood to another. Very quickly, they can go from being calm, polite and charming to physically lashing out. They may be cuddling people one minute and then punching them the next. Sometimes, acquaintances will be amazed at stories of a child's extreme state, when they may only have ever seen them in their delightful, angelic state. Triggers for mood swings could be anything, but often demands, transitioning from one thing to another and taking away or removing something they are fixated on can cause a flashpoint. Parents become quite adept at knowing how to manage transitions and reducing demands, but dealing with 'obsessions' can be really problematic. Children and young people with PDA can become fascinated with anything at any time. Their obsessions may be with just inanimate objects or a particular subject, but often it can be with a particular person. This fascination with other children can be so strong that it can be extremely difficult for the other child. 'One-way' invitations to tea are common as other parents recognise the controlling and overbearing effect the child with PDA can have on other children, and all but a few close friends may remain. If they share interests with the friends, such as computer games and TV characters (e.g. Doctor Who), then this can help. As children grow older, their behaviour can be seen as immature by their peers.

Role playing appears to come very easily to the child with PDA. It can be used to advantage sometimes to disguise a demand (e.g. 'Shall we be SpongeBob and Patrick hunting jellyfish on our way back to the car?', rather than simply asking the child to leave the playground). Sometimes it's helpful for parents to remember quotes from favourite DVDs to 'pull out of the bag' at opportune moments to defuse a situation. Some children with PDA do become very intensely involved in their role playing. They can become so involved in taking on a role or character that the lines between reality and fantasy can blur. Sometimes they can find it difficult to come out of the fantasy role. One parent recalls her son 'being' Steven Gerrard, the England footballer, for three days during which she had to address him as Steven and have his 'manager' come for dinner! Another parent describes her daughter as being so interested in *The Lion King* that in response to demands, she sometimes transforms herself into Nala, growling and lashing out at other children quite ferociously.

Parents often ask, 'Should we indulge our child's fascinations?'. There is no easy answer to this and it will depend on the topic or the nature of their interest. Assuming it is not a harmful interest or one which puts a child at risk, a good question to ask is, 'Can I use it to engage and motivate my child?' For example, a child who finds going to the dentist particularly difficult may be motivated by a reward related to their current interest. Linking co-operation with a reward can be a helpful strategy, but there other considerations which can affect the family dynamics. For instance, parents often comment that rewards which are effective for their child with PDA need to be more tangible and immediate than those they use for their children who do not have PDA. Sometimes this can mean that rewards which are used to motivate a child with PDA can be expensive (such as a book or toy rather than just a sticker from the dentist's drawer). Sometimes children with PDA can try to take advantage of the offer of a reward and pressurise their parents into bigger prizes than are appropriate to the 'deal'. Obviously, parents need to be aware that this approach should be used sparingly if other methods fail, or for particularly difficult situations that are very necessary, such as visiting the dentist, since getting into a pattern of 'bribing' the child to do everything is unhelpful. Parents will also need to use their creativity to avert any difficulties which arise among siblings who may feel that the rewards they receive as siblings are not as extravagant. In addition, although using rewards can be effective for some children with PDA, the anticipation of either 'winning' or 'losing' a reward can become a perceived pressure in itself. Specific reward systems may work for short periods but are less likely to be as enduring as with children with autism.

Some obsessions are stress relieving for the child, but obviously if the strong interest is inappropriate, unhealthy or dangerous then it may be wise to try to divert that interest into something more appropriate, healthy or safe. A fascination for instance with ice, where the child loves the feel of the ice and loves smashing it and holding it would be unsafe and inappropriate if they were constantly trying to get on to a frozen pond, but perhaps filling up containers with water to make various amounts or types of ice to play with somewhere else is a better option. Parents need to try to think laterally all the time and try to work out different options and alternatives for behaviour that is unwanted or unhelpful.

MANAGING DEMANDS IN THE HOME

The principles of management within the home are the same as the principles of management at school. The strategies used there, which have been detailed in Chapter 2, can be applied here too. There are differences, of course, in that teachers must work within the structure of the school day, whereas there is obviously much more variation in a home situation. Often there are extended family members who also look after the child, and this sometimes leads to conflicting styles of managing a child. While different approaches may be well intentioned, the child's well-being must be at the centre, which provides another good reason for a clear diagnosis, so that those caring for the child can all understand the reasons behind the behaviour and then try to implement strategies together.

Before diagnosis, parents will already have worked out what seems effective to get their child to do what they are asked. They may not have realised *why* it works though. Many parents have commented on how much easier things became once they realised that it was the demands, not the task itself, that seemed to cause much of the anxiety. They certainly recognise that the child desperately wants or needs to be in control.

Parenting style

REDUCING DEMANDS

Reducing demands at times when the child seems less tolerant is an obvious strategy, once parents realise that the demands themselves are causing the problem. Reducing demands does not mean letting the child do what they want all the time. It means keeping the demands synchronised with what the child can cope with at that moment in time, and presenting requests in a way the child can tolerate. Reducing demands works best if requests can be made in a flexible way, that is, in a way which leaves room for manoeuvre in case there needs to be some re-negotiation. If a request is made in a rigid way, then it is hard to reduce or modify the terms of it without someone losing face.

DISGUISING DEMANDS

Disguising demands or taking an indirect approach to demands is good way of 'asking without asking'. For example, making a game out of getting socks on or 'I can't quite see how this shirt buttons up, can you help me?', 'I think I need your help finding your socks'. Some parents use a 'reverse psychology approach' – for example, 'You can't eat all that... No way I don't believe you!' A slightly more subtle way might be, 'Oh James?...[pause]... Oh, actually no it's OK...[pause and gauge interest]... Well I was going to ask you to do X but I know you don't really like doing that so it's OK...' This sometimes appeals to the child because it offers them the opportunity to take the lead, be in control and be unexpectedly helpful. Initially, it may seem difficult to go against more conventional parenting techniques because they are comfortable and familiar to most adults. It can be highly effective, though, to change how parents parent. Besides, many find that they had already been implementing strategies which suit children with PDA. Sometimes just having the knowledge that what they are doing is the right approach can be a relief for parents who have long been told that they must be firmer. Although it takes a while to get used to, the result can be a calmer and easier child.

DISTRACTION

Distraction is another simple technique which can be used, particularly when a child is younger. Often, simple demands like getting dressed can be achieved while chatting to the child about something they enjoy or are fully engaged in conversing about. One parent described how she can get her child to put his clothes on and get ready in the morning if she just carries on reading to him. He is so engaged in listening to the story that he automatically gets on with the task in hand. Equally, using this technique can be a helpful way of distracting from the pressures of a transition (such as from home to the car, leaving a game to come for a meal), by starting a conversation that will intrigue the child, then keeping it going as the adult starts to leave one place and move to the next. Often the child with PDA, once sufficiently engaged, will follow without needing to draw attention to the transition.

OFFERING CHOICES

Parents will find things that work for their child. As they get older, children and young people with PDA may become more adept at realising what parents are doing. They may become more avoidant in different ways and then different strategies may be required. Instead of asking a child to get his shoes on, for example, a parent might ask him if he would like to wear the brown shoes or the black shoes today, or might ask him if he would like to put his shoes on in the living room or by the door and so *offering choices* may be a more realistic way of presenting the demand. It is worth remembering that over time, children's own motivations change so what was a problem at one time will probably fade and be replaced by a different challenge.

IGNORING UNDESIRABLE BEHAVIOUR

Swearing and being rude is an effective strategy for a child or young person with PDA to use on his parents, and how parents manage this may determine the outcomes. Generally, swearing may be less damaging than violence but it is still undesirable, and reacting very little to it may often be the best plan. There may be other considerations too for families where younger siblings are exposed to vocabulary that parents would prefer they did not learn.

Similarly, older siblings may feel frustrated if there is, understandably, a different parental reaction if they were to swear or act rudely, compared to the one that their brother or sister with PDA receives. Sometimes difficulties will be managed best by *choosing to ignore some undesirable behaviour*, in the light of having selected other priorities. Although parents may know that reacting against the undesirable behaviour does not help the situation, human nature dictates that no one can be perfect all the time. Parents should not feel at fault if they have reacted badly themselves, but they should try to learn from their experiences. While their child's behaviour may be difficult to accept, their response to it is also important. It can mean that they too need to develop strategies for coping with their own levels of frustration.

FLEXIBILITY AND ADAPTABILITY

Parents will need *flexibility* and *adaptability* when parenting their child with PDA. Their child may often be very inflexible and find it difficult to adapt so the parents will need to practise being flexible themselves to accommodate this. For example, a plan to go out for the afternoon may be quickly abandoned and a different plan adopted when a child with PDA perhaps has an unexpected outburst. It's a well-prepared parent who has a Plan B or a 'get-out clause'. Building an 'emergency exit' to any family outing is always worth considering, but changing arrangements that were anticipated can also have an impact on siblings, which needs to be taken into account. Siblings of children with PDA often learn themselves about the need for being flexible, but it can lead to resentment if their needs and expectations are not accommodated somewhere. In Julie Davies' (1993) booklet for brothers and sisters of children with PDA, one sibling says of his sister, 'When we go to the shops, she says "I'm not going" so one of mum or dad has to stay.' Whereas this is indeed often the reality, siblings need to have time and space to express their opinions and emotions so that their well-being is protected and so that they can contribute to solutions that work for their family.

DE-PERSONALISING DEMANDS

It is helpful for any child to have some structure to their day and a basic routine which makes them feel safe. Often children with an autism spectrum disorder need a tight, structured routine in their day. Routines which classically work so well for children with autism often cause friction for children with PDA. However, structure does have some benefit in that it can *de-personalise the demand*. Demands can be 'concealed' within the structure of a routine, which de-personalises the pressure of the request. For example, rather than saying 'I want you to get ready for bed now', to be able to say, 'Oh, look at the time! It's time to get ready for bed' can make a subtle, yet effective, difference.

For some families and some situations, using visual systems can help in this respect. For example, having a visual list of what to get ready for school the next day can make information clear without linking the demand to a personal request. Having a jovial personality and an ability to think quickly helps, but after a long day of difficult behaviour, insults or aggressive outbursts, this is not always achievable! Another way of de-personalising the demand is by saying something is a rule (e.g. government policy, or the rules of the tenancy, etc). This takes the onus away from the parent. Using pictures of things as a visual cue in the home (e.g. a picture by the bathroom sink of someone – possibly themselves – brushing their teeth) may help to de-personalise the demand.

STAYING CALM AND NEUTRAL

'Keep calm and carry on', the famous expression used by the UK government during World War Two as part of their public morale-boosting posters, has been referred to by several parents when describing how to handle bouts of difficult or aggressive behaviour. It is really important to try to *stay calm and neutral*, although that's not easy, at times, for most parents. When parenting a child with PDA, the levels of stress can rise much higher, much more quickly. Using a soft tone of voice in the household will encourage your child to do the same. Shouting is likely to increase the 'excitement' for the child with PDA and can 'encourage' them to use this type of behaviour more. What is more, if a child with PDA gets the sense that the adults caring for them are unsure of what to do next, or are becoming agitated themselves, this will have an impact on their reaction. They may start to also feel anxious about what will happen next, but they may also spot an opportunity to insist on their own agenda if they feel that the circumstances are open to re-negotiation.

DEALING WITH BEDTIME DIFFICULTIES

Many parents of children with additional needs report difficulties regarding bedtimes. Parents of some children with ASDs who enjoy rule-based approaches, may find once they establish a bedtime routine, and as long as it is not altered, there are fewer difficulties getting children to bed. This is not likely to be the case for children with PDA, and bedtime can be a slot of the day which is fraught for many families. There are a number of requests and expectations associated with bedtimes, and there are inevitably other issues affecting parents too. There may be other siblings that parents are also trying to settle to sleep, plus of course, bedtime falling at the end of the day, may mean that parents themselves are tired and more emotional. One parent writing on the PDA Contact Group's online forum said:

Bedtime is tough in our house and causes many meltdowns and we battle to get our son into bed at a sensible time. If he is in a highly resistant mood, we often find that if we do not badger him to get to bed he will fall asleep on the sofa. We leave him to sleep for a while and then wake him and suggest he will be more comfortable in bed. He will usually comply. He gets to bed later than we would like, but earlier than if we had a major tantrum.

Some of the following strategies may be helpful to families who regularly have difficulties around bedtime:

- Consider any sensory issues which may be getting in the way of the child either co-operating or settling. For example, make sure that pyjamas are not too 'scratchy' and that their blankets/duvet are a suitable size and weight for them. Make sure their room is warm/cool enough and dark/light enough. Getting these details right will at least remove any easily solved problems.

- Choose priorities; for example, if they are resistant to pyjamas for whatever reason, can they sleep in a big T-shirt? Or if they prefer to make a 'den' bed on the floor, can they sleep in this? Once priorities have been chosen, try not to get distracted away from these, and actively to choose to drop other issues.

- Use distraction or de-personalised ways of presenting a request. For instance, use a timer to measure how quickly a child can get ready for bed; read a story to distract from the transition between playing and getting into bed; start brushing teeth in the kitchen and keep brushing as you walk to the bathroom in order to ensure they have brushed for long enough.

- Give the child as much control and choice as possible, such as in what order they complete their 'bedtime tasks'; which colour toothbrush they use; which book is read to them or which activity they do just before bed, or in bed.

- Consider using visual strategies, such as a schedule of photos, symbols or written words as a prompt, rather than the adult's instructions. This technique can work if it appeals to the child's sense of humour or interest – for example, pictures of a favourite character going to bed, slapstick photographs of themselves or a parent, getting ready for bed in the 'wrong' way such as using a toothbrush to brush their hair, or putting their arms into pyjama trousers.

- Simply making their room an enjoyable place to be, can be helpful. Some parents change the bedroom round frequently, using novelty as a technique to maintain interest. Making a 'my time' box full of things they find comforting they can choose at bedtime, such as listening to music or a story, etc., can help ease the transition to being by themselves in bed. Some parents may find their child will only settle with a particular routine or comfort that they have specified. Parents may have to experiment with different things, and those things may only work for short periods of time, but going back to ones they have used before is also helpful.

While some of the techniques in common sleep problem books may also help the child with PDA, it is often necessary to consider how the 'control' differs for these children. One child described difficulties he had falling asleep in three different ways. First, he was aware that while he slept, the world carries on. This may include his parents having conversations or making decisions that he wanted to know about or influence, but would not be able to if he were asleep. Second, he was at the mercy of whatever dreams, good or bad, he would have and was uncomfortable with not being able to control what he dreamed about. Third, he found the moment of actually falling asleep very anxiety-provoking and would resist the process of 'letting go' to fall asleep. These comments highlight a very different perspective regarding difficult behaviour at bedtime, to the typically developing child.

Parents may need much perseverance, ingenuity and patience. Some parents, despite trying many strategies, still get no respite at bedtimes. There is some evidence that melatonin, a drug which mimics the body's natural sleep-inducing hormone, can be helpful for sleep problems in autism spectrum disorders. Despite some licensing issues in the UK, there are a number of paediatricians who prescribe it for use with children on the autism spectrum, with some positive results.

Choosing priorities

It may be helpful to try to work on one or two home problems at a time, and *choose priorities* about what the adults are going to accept for the time being, while they tackle that particular problem. For instance, if a child has difficulty getting ready for school, and the parent has decided to prioritise that particular difficulty, they may decide to let other less pressing challenges go, such as swearing. These priorities will be very specific to individual families.

A parent from the PDA Contact Group forum commented:

With all the problems I have with her, to keep my sanity, I prioritise what's a problem. I don't mind the grazing (eating) because it's not that important in my opinion compared to other things, and for my own sanity, I let a lot of things go. As for the getting dressed for school, that's very important.

Table 3.1 Priority rating chart (home)

Prioritising behaviour – How important is it that she…?	Priority rating	Comments and context
does not hurt herself	1	*Non-negotiable – will be prevented from doing so.*
does not hurt other people (non-accidentally)	1	*Non-negotiable – will be prevented from doing so.*
comes shopping with the rest of the family	3	*Except for going to shoe shop as required (with extra adult).*
brushes her teeth twice daily	2	*Once daily is sufficient – also working on reducing sweets.*
showers/baths daily	2	*Once a week is a requirement but she can choose which day.*
has household chores	3	*Have agreed a separate arrangement with her siblings to make it fair for them.*
has a fixed bedtime	3	*Agreed time to stay in bedroom without electronic toys/screen.*
has pocket money	3	*Agreed amount as basic (adjustments can be made re additional money if earned).*
attends after school activities	3	*Not a priority at the moment but keep discussing this.*
copes with a babysitter/ childminder	1	*Agreed different boundaries for babysitter to make this acceptable to us all.*
has a hobby	2	*Interest in drama important to pursue for hobby, social opportunity and self-confidence.*
keeps her bedroom tidy	3	*Not a priority.*
accepts that some days her brother or sister has a chance to choose what we do/watch on TV	1	*Will give notice when this will happen – however hard, it is non-negotiable because of siblings' well-being.*
does not damage property	1	*Non-negotiable – will be prevented from doing so.*
gets out of bed in the morning (school days)	2	*School will accept her up to 30 minutes late without insisting on full uniform being worn.*
gets out of bed in the morning (not school day)	3	*Not a priority at the moment.*
feels valued and accepted	1	*Obviously! So need to work positively with her and openly with others involved.*
Any other category which is a priority for my child at this time?		

Priority rating:
1 = high priority in all circumstances
2 = highly desirable but not essential
3 = low priority – we need to work around this another way

Set out in Table 3.1 is a priority table which might be used at home, like that used in school in Chapter 2 (p.49). It shows a list of priority ratings, alongside behaviours, with comments, and of course will be tailored to the individual child. The principle here, is that there are simply too many issues to address simultaneously. Therefore, families need to discuss and decide which are current priorities and why, so that they can co-ordinate their efforts to work on these together.

MANAGING AGGRESSION AND MELTDOWNS

Not every child or young person with PDA will use extreme behaviours, but many do display aggressive, outspoken and violent tendencies as a result of their anxiety-driven need to control. Some will also have explosive episodes of panic, or meltdowns, which have been discussed in Chapter 2. Sometimes these behaviours can include self-harm, which presents a slightly different challenge. There may be issues overlapping with self-esteem here, but using self-injurious behaviour is extremely difficult for adults, especially parents, to ignore, and from this perspective is a highly effective demand-avoidance strategy. This section does show some extreme examples of what can occur, but these are not by any means typical of every child with PDA. In addition, children may go through various stages within their development and cope more or less well at different times of their life, often depending on many elements of their circumstances, including hormone changes. Equally, their behaviour at school is often very different from behaviour at home.

Meltdowns can last for literally hours and be utterly exhausting, demoralising and very destructive for everyone concerned, so avoiding the meltdowns becomes a major goal in a household with a child with PDA. This can make parents feel like they are 'walking on eggshells' all the time. Meltdowns, unlike tantrums, can go on for hours. They are not attention-seeking behaviour and it can often be impossible to simply distract the child out of them. They indicate an anxiety-fuelled loss of control, not a determined and organised effort to 'get their own way'. Usually, the child will have lost all reasoning. Even as toddlers they appear to gain immense anger and incredible strength during these meltdowns. One parent described how she had to have her son's room reinforced because he was so destructive during his violent behaviour. This would, at its worst, include kicking, hitting, biting, punching, and throwing missiles. This apparent intent to harm is not a willful or deliberate act but, in that moment, the child or young person feels that they have no option but to react like this.

It is helpful to see these meltdowns as 'panic attacks'. Realising that pushing demands could lead to this kind of outburst, will have an impact on how any adult interacts with a child with PDA. When this kind of attack happens, a parent will need to 'ride it out' in as calm and as reassuring a way as possible, while keeping those around them, including the child, safe. This is often easier said than done, and the additional stress it places on family life should not be underestimated. Reducing demands generally on children with PDA, or perhaps re-phrasing and disguising the demands, can reduce the number of meltdowns a child has. Sometimes there are warning signs with some children that things are becoming difficult for them. It may be a look or a facial expression that provides a signal that the child is becoming increasingly agitated or anxious. Maybe the child puts his hood up and folds his arms when he is starting to struggle. This can alert a parent who then needs to stay calm and try to help him.

De-escalating techniques

Offering reassurance that everything will be OK and encouraging children to explain their fears or concerns as they happen, can help. Parents may need to avoid firing too many questions at this time, though, because the child's processing, as well as their co-operation, will be compromised. Processing information in the build-up to a rage becomes very much reduced, so a simple 'What's up?' may be all that can be asked. Kay and Haitham Al-Ghani have written a children's picture book illustrating exactly this point. In their book *The Red Beast* (2008) there is a monster who changes when he is upset. His mouth becomes bigger and his ears become smaller; that is, he becomes more outspoken and aggressive at the same time as he is less able to listen and understand. It can also be helpful to everyone concerned, assuming it is safe to do so, if some time and space can be offered to allow an opportunity to calm and re-adjust.

There are some other useful strategies outlined in Kari Dunn Buron and Mitzi Curtis'sbook *The Incredible 5-Point Scale* (2003). Encouraging children to use a scale of 1 to 5, it offers ways children can indicate how angry they feel, which can be a good way for children to communicate with parents the degree of emotion they are feeling. It also suggests developing a list of agreed responses which are appropriate to the scale of the feeling or the situation. At times away from the point of crisis, parents and children can agree some acceptable responses to a given number on the scale. The next stage is to work on what can be done to bring the number scale down; for example, in recognition of the fact that a child reached number 5 at the dinner table, they were taken to their bedroom. Following this, there need to be strategies which can help to move them from that 5 towards a 2 or 3. This needs to happen before a resolution can be applied or negotiated regarding the cause of the explosive behaviour. These are known as *de-escalating techniques*. They may include relaxation techniques, distraction using current interests or physical exercise. It can also be really helpful for children who have meltdowns to help them to expend energy in a good way at various points throughout the day. This could be as a sport that they like such as, bike riding, trampolining or playing in the park. Parents may find that doing this expends so much energy that they then don't 'need' to get rid of it in a negative way later on. In addition, this may offer parent and child another positive activity that they can do together. There is also evidence to endorse the positive effects of exercise on mood for everyone. Developing a selection of strategies needs to be worked on at either a calm time, when something mild irritates them, or if talking about a previous meltdown.

Discussing meltdowns afterwards can be helpful if a child is prepared to talk about them. Be aware though that some parents report that their children seem to revert to the angry mood they were in just by talking about it, especially if the 'problem' or 'issue' wasn't resolved or identified. In this case, it may be better to wait a day or two before discussing it. Alternatively, parents could try de-personalising the discussion by using examples from characters on a familiar TV show or puppets to illustrate the point.

Meltdowns in public

Meltdowns at home are bad enough, but meltdowns in public places are more difficult times for families. There is the added pressure of the parent feeling they should 'do what is expected of them as a parent', and the feeling that many people are watching them and disapproving of how they deal with the situation. There may be a feeling that onlookers are thinking 'what that child needs is a good smack'. Alongside this is the effect that this kind of situation may be having on siblings. This is where the parent must try to develop a very thick skin, which some people find easier than others. Parents need to try to remember that *their* child responds better to the techniques *they* have discovered, for *their* child, not the standard ones. They should try to stay calm and try to stay in a positive frame of mind. If they are able to weigh up the situation then they should do so. 'Is my child safe?', 'Are other people safe?', 'What are the priorities for my child and my family at this time?'. If they are able to work out the reason for the meltdown, then they should try to reassure the child. If the meltdown happens, for example, because the parent said 'No' to something in particular, consider the possibility of shifting the goalposts by compromising.

It is important to try to reserve definite 'No' responses to those situations which are genuinely non-negotiable. This can avoid becoming involved in unnecessary dilemmas regarding backing down on an issue that actually was not a real priority after all. Sometimes parents feel they have said 'No' to something they cannot go back on. There may be good reasons for sticking to these decisions, such as, safety, unfairness for siblings, financial constraints, etc. If they know that saying 'No' is likely to result in a meltdown, then they could try to think of an alternative way of presenting their decision, or a compromise, or be prepared to take the meltdown. They need to weigh up what is worth a meltdown and what is not, and that may change for different situations. They may feel strongly about not buying their child a new toy every time they go to the supermarket, but they may also know that often meltdowns happen at the supermarket, and that buying new toys can avert them. Working out a compromise is something parents can think about at home when they have time and space. They may come to a decision, for example, that they will continue to buy new toys at the supermarket, but they will set a price limit, and they will do something comparable for siblings, at a different time. To make decisions during a meltdown in a public place requires parents to think very quickly and calmly, which is not easy. With a typically developing child one could say 'No' and even if they have a tantrum, it's ignored and then they come round. Over time, it also becomes less likely that they will repeat the tantrum. With a child with PDA if one says 'No' and they have a meltdown and the parent ignores it, it may last for hours; plus, it may not affect the chances of preventing it happening again another day. In extreme circumstances they may damage the shop, threaten or perform violence on others, resulting in both parent and child being thrown out of the shop or, worse, involving security or police. They may then end up having to explain that the child has a disability and cannot help his behaviour, all at the same time that their child continues to be upset and potentially unsafe. Being at constant risk of things developing into this sort of situation is what some parents with a child with PDA have to deal with regularly. Finding a compromise and deciding what is not 'worth' the meltdown for these parents, becomes a necessary method to use if they feel a situation is developing. This is *not* a 'cop-out' or poor parenting. This is taking the most responsible course of action in order to reduce their anxiety and to allow everyone to get home safely, possibly without, but preferably with, the shopping.

Surviving meltdowns

Meltdowns sometimes give no warning. Parents may have used all the recommended techniques yet meltdowns will still happen. As time goes on, and they use these techniques more often, the frequency of the meltdowns should reduce. It is important to recognise that seeing through a meltdown can also be a positive experience. It can be bonding to deal with a difficult meltdown and to be able to reflect on having got through it together. It can also offer an opportunity to reinforce that bond by moving on to something positive afterwards. Looking back on the detail of how it was handled, in a moment that is appropriate, can allow everyone a chance to reflect on the way both the child and the parent have handled it. Children with PDA often have their own ideas about how they or the parents could have helped to reduce their anxiety, so it's important that parents listen to their suggestions. Putting the child's suggestions into action may not always be feasible or reasonable, but they still need to be heard, and this will give the child a feeling of some control and influence over the situation. Often though, the flashpoint can reflect a sudden mood swing that takes even the child with PDA by surprise. A parent using the PDA Contact Group forum writes:

We felt we had to call 999 after Alex had us held in the kitchen at knife point. This is our little boy, the little boy who holds our hand on the way to school despite his peers laughing at him, the little boy who will tell his mum she's beautiful just 'because you're my mum'. This is also the little boy who will kiss & cuddle his younger sister & say he loves her one minute, then, in the bat of an eye, he'll pull her hair & slap her face.

Finding a way for the adults involved to get support themselves after a meltdown is really important too. Some parents report feeling very down for a few days after a meltdown. While often the child or young person with PDA is able to draw a line under the episode, it can be hard for parents to do so, especially if the meltdown has triggered additional meetings or other agencies getting involved, and so, parents need to find something which helps them recover from difficult incidents too.

Some children can feel remorse for what they have done after a meltdown, especially if there are noticeable outcomes (e.g. someone is bleeding or items are broken), and this can lead to low self-esteem. Children with PDA may look at the results around them after an outburst and feel upset that it happened. However, they may struggle to recognise the chain of events which led them to explode, and to recall the series of actions during the meltdown. This makes it hard for them to understand why it happened, as well as to predict how they could prevent a similar situation in the future. In some cases, the aggression can become so bad that families reach crisis. Some parents have reported having to lock up household hazards, such as sharp knives, to keep them out of the child's reach during a meltdown. Some have called the police because they felt so unsafe, even regarding young children. Involving the police is unlikely to be helpful, but shows the point some parents reach in asking for help. Unfortunately, some families will have broken down completely and, in extreme cases, children have been placed into care. This highlights the need for better understanding and support for these children and their families. One parent using the PDA Contact Group forum reported:

Things all came to a head with my 9-year-old daughter who has PDA the other evening when I had something she wanted. When I said that she could not have it she tried kicking, punching and biting me. I remained calm and still said no. She then reached into the kitchen drawer and got out a pair of scissors and tried to stab me in the hand with them. I was so shocked I gave in to her straight away. I spoke to her later when she had calmed down. She understood what she had done but was totally unable to control herself. I am now starting to get really worried about what she will do next.

GOOD DAYS

It's easy to forget when describing some of the more extreme and distressing circumstances, that children with PDA are also often incredibly charming and appealing. They can be engaging company with children and adults alike. Many parents say their children can sometimes have totally happy and carefree days. When children with PDA are relaxed and happy, and not anxious, they can be some of the most polite and pleasant children one could meet. Younger children can be drawn to a child with PDA as they are often lively, energetic and fun. Parents describe how other people have commented on how charming their child with PDA can be. Indeed being charming is also a way of being in control too, although it is a much more pleasurable one. Children with PDA are often extremely likeable, and it is perhaps true that some show only this aspect of their character until they get to know another person better. When a child feels 'safe' enough with an adult, more of the less desirable features of PDA can show themselves. This is often true for the start of a new term, with a new teacher, a new friend or a new situation and can sometimes be seen as the 'honeymoon period'. When this happens, it is fortunate that the child has built some positive history with the people around them as this can strengthen the relationships which help to get through the tougher times. It is certainly important that adults make the most of these honeymoon periods to build rapport with children with PDA.

The aim of this book is to help parents and professionals who work directly with children and young people to realise that difficult behaviours stem from anxiety, and not from willful opposition. By reducing these anxieties and managing them better, there will be more good days, children will develop more strategies themselves, and will be better prepared for their adult life. As has already been referred to, Ross Greene in *The Explosive Child* (2005) reiterates that it should be assumed that 'children do well if they can' given the right help, support and opportunities.

RELATIONSHIPS WITHIN THE HOME

Effect on the family as a whole

Giving a child a diagnosis of PDA, or ASD for that matter too, will inevitably have an impact on their parents. There is commonly a period of 'grieving' for the child that parents had anticipated having, as they adjust to a different outlook. It can be a troubled time for parents, when they will question everything they themselves have done and could have done differently. Of course, a developmental condition is something they have no control over, and yet, even when they have the diagnosis, it is common for parents to carry some sort of responsibility and struggle to free themselves from a degree of guilt. Life then opens on a new chapter, coming to terms with the reality of the child they have got, rather than the one they had envisaged. This process affects individuals in very different ways and is one that parents go through in their own way, at their own pace. It is a time when support services, parent groups and understanding friends and family can make all the difference.

Parenting a child with PDA can be very tiring because being with someone who is unpredictable means staying in a state of high-alert all the time, on the look-out for the next potential flashpoint. It is not unusual for parents of children with additional needs to experience significant episodes of depression, associated with high levels of unpredictability, anxiety and exhaustion. This, in turn, can impact on parents' own social lives and network of support. One parent using the PDA Contact Group forum, writes:

It has brought home to me how we have lost regular contact with our friends and family. I suddenly realised I have not seen friends we used to see once a month, since New Years Eve. I know most of it is my fault as I am so absorbed in caring for Leslie, and managing his behaviour, but they too must have made a decision not to get together. I don't know if they're trying not to bother me, finding it hard to talk to me about Leslie, or whether they have consciously distanced themselves.

Parents may need regular respite from their child with PDA in order to re-group, to re-charge their batteries and to have some time when their other children, or indeed they themselves, take priority. They may, however, have a difficult time getting respite from their child with PDA. From the perspective of the child, they may find it hard to join some of the local out-of-school activities which are available to other children, and these services need to be adapted to meet the needs of children with PDA.

If available and willing, grandparents may be able to offer some help in looking after the child on occasion, but as the child becomes older and stronger, they may feel less able to do so. Some family members or friends may avoid helping out if they have experienced a difficult outburst and decide that they cannot manage the child at all. Out-of-school clubs and holiday playschemes may also find the level of explosive behaviour in some children or young people with PDA too challenging.

Sometimes, when families do set up suitable respite care arrangements, the child may put up such resistance to going, that parents may decide that their lives would be easier without the respite after all. Often parents become so used to understanding how their child 'operates' that they do not trust anyone else to be able to care for them without risking major consequences. Some children with PDA are able to 'hold things together' while they are being cared for by other people, but then things come crashing down once they get back home. These are not easy situations to manage, but they do not mean it is not worth persevering with respite care. There are obvious benefits to siblings, offering them time when their needs are clearly prioritised over their brother or sister with PDA. There can be benefits too to sustaining marriages and relationships. Plus, over time, and dealt with sensitively, most children with PDA can become accustomed to, and comfortable with, spending some time with people other than those within the immediate family. Indeed, as they get older, this also becomes more appropriate to their age. The Autism Education Trust (2008, p.100) review of current practice comments:

> It is very important for children and young people on the autism spectrum to have ways in which they can use their time constructively out of school hours. They need to have positive experiences with peers and adults. Without support, they are likely to spend large amounts of time on their own and/or within the family home at an age when others are going out with friends or attending clubs and leisure activities.

Relationships between parents can suffer due to the added stresses and strains of bringing up a child with PDA. Family support, relationship counselling and social services can offer extremely valuable help to families at various points in time. Systems enabling access to these services will obviously vary according to different regions, and will alter over time. Parents should remember, though, that they do not need to cope alone, and have a right to whatever support their local area is able to provide.

A parent using the PDA Contact Group forum commented on applying for additional funding:

...you get used to bending over backwards with everything and walking on eggshells. Basically, you can't relax and can never assume things are going to be OK. Something that's good one day can be a disaster the next. If you look at isolated moments it could read that your child doesn't have a problem but if you look at the ground work, preparation, quick-thinking, and shoring up that has to happen to make something at least have a chance of going OK, then you're seeing the real picture. It's so easy to forget all that because you do it without thinking.

In addition, there are a number of welfare benefits available (again, depending on area and current funding), which parents can look into accessing. This is not only to allow for the direct additional costs associated with having a child with a disability in a family, but the indirect costs too, such as the increased likelihood that both parents are unable to work. The Autism Education Trust review (2008, p.40) mentions that:

> Autism can be a factor in moving families down the income ladder. Having a child on the autism spectrum has been shown to depress the earning potential of families…it is believed that families coping with someone on the autism spectrum face a higher rate of breakdown than other families… Lone parents are also less likely to have a built-in support system…to rely on for support and advice.

Despite the time it takes to fill out the forms for welfare benefits, it is worth applying for. Many parents feel that they shouldn't apply because 'some days he seems like any regular kid' or because they worry that 'people might think badly of me for claiming disability benefits when there are so many other kids with physical disabilities'. Parents need to remind themselves of the huge amount of work they do daily to avoid outbursts and anxiety, as well as the toll it takes on their family when outbursts are unavoidable.

Effect on siblings

The behaviours of a child or young person with PDA has implications for other members of the family. Siblings of children with PDA can be under a huge amount of pressure. It can become commonplace for them to have to cope with making regular adaptations to allow for the additional demands of living with a sibling with PDA. Sometimes, though, they feel close to the child with PDA and understand them better than their parents. They may come across as less threatening to the child with PDA than their parents, so the siblings may find they can get their brother or sister with PDA to do things their parents cannot. As one sibling said: 'I'm better at dealing with him because I'm a kid as well.'

They may also, though, be on the receiving end of verbal or physical aggression too. Siblings can become unhappy and resentful, and parents need to try to make time for them. There will invariably be one set of rules for the child with PDA and another set of rules for the sibling. This can feel very unfair for the sibling if the condition is not explained properly, and the sibling's own ideas and concerns are not taken into account.

Siblings need to be able to express that it can be unfair, and to feel that it is OK to be angry themselves sometimes. One parent on the PDA Contact Group forum said:

I do also allow his brother 'private' whinge time when I make clear that it is OK to feel embarrassed or fed up about having a brother with PDA sometimes, and that his parents get frustrated too.

Brushing these feelings under the carpet is likely to result in resentment on the part of the siblings. Talking about these issues openly can nonetheless be emotional and sometimes challenging for parents too. There is such an overwhelming pressure on parents, and it can be easy to expect a lot from brothers and sisters, but good communication between the parents and siblings and quality time spent with all the children can help. Many families are able to organise the logistics of this by separating and doing different activities with the children. Whereas this may work well at a practical level, it does not provide time with both parents together, which is something that many siblings express a wish for. The alternative, though, necessitates finding child care for the child with PDA, which may not be straightforward. One sibling commented: 'When we go to the shops, she says, "I'm not going" so one of Mum or Dad has to stay.'

It is important to discuss with the siblings why their brother or sister behaves in the way they do and what sort of things can help make the whole family's life easier. It is important for the sibling to understand triggers and to be able use helpful strategies too, while recognising the pressure they too are under. The child or young person with PDA can be literally dictating how things need to be, and it is this controlling nature which can be incredibly overbearing for other children. Prioritising siblings, and giving them some influence within the family is helpful, and will enable them to feel they are important too. Parents can all too easily 'forget' the needs of siblings, not intentionally of course, but because their child with PDA is usually more dominant within the family, and because the siblings are usually more adaptable. Sometimes engineering situations so that siblings have some time to be themselves, choose the programme on the TV, choose what they are having for dinner, choose which toothpaste they buy for a change, etc. can make all the difference, as it is often these little things that are 'controlled' every day by the child with PDA and that can affect the daily lives of siblings to such an extent that they can themselves become low in mood and self-esteem. From time to time, families may need to consider letting a sibling's choice override that of the child with PDA, as long as dealing with seeing this through is safe and achievable, in order to illustrate fairness.

For some children with PDA, rewards for positive behaviour may need to be larger than one might expect for children without PDA. If this is not handled carefully, it can lead to sibling jealousy. One way around this may be to reward the siblings at the same time, acknowledging that although one is already able to go to the dentist without a fuss, for instance, it is nonetheless appreciated. This also means that when the child with PDA makes positive steps, there are rewards or benefits for all the family. It can be helpful to develop rewards within the family which are related to 'special time' to do a particular activity rather than a 'prize' the value of which can be measured in monetary terms. It is important for parents to remind the siblings about the positive aspects of their brother or sister with PDA too, so they are not just placing the focus on the negative aspects. A sibling commented on their sister, saying: 'We act videos together – she's very good at that.'

Parents should remember that it can be very isolating for the siblings, as their peers may have no idea just how difficult the situation is at home, and inviting friends over may not be advisable. Equally, siblings may feel embarrassed when their brother or sister is rude or aggressive in public. Questions they may not have answers to include: What and how do they tell their friends about their brother or sister? Does anyone they know live with a sibling with additional needs? What can they do at home to make things easier for themselves? Their sibling with PDA? Their parents? Sibling groups can be incredibly helpful in this respect.

Some support services or local charities run siblings groups which meet regularly. Sometimes these groups are short term and have a clear focus on helping siblings to understand more about their brother or sister's needs, to introduce them to other children living in similar situations, and to help them to develop some coping strategies for themselves. Other groups meet with a more sociable focus, mainly helping siblings to make contact with other children who are dealing with similar issues to their own, plus supporting discussions on occasion. The advantages for siblings of accessing these kinds of group are to help them to feel less isolated, to help them understand more about their brother or sister, and to offer them strategies which may help. At siblings groups, they do not have to explain what living with a sibling with PDA is like, because they are among other children who already know. They may feel more able to chat to peers with similar family circumstances than to those at mainstream school, or to their parents, who will also be finding the situation very stressful, or to other adults who do not know their family.

In the booklet *Children with Pathological Demand Avoidance Syndrome: A Booklet for Brothers and Sisters* (Davies 2003) there is a lot of helpful information and guidance for children over seven. It details with common questions asked by siblings of children with PDA.

Julie Davies (1994) has also written a document called *Brothers and Sisters of Children with Autism: A Checklist of Things to Do or Consider for Their Support*. Within this, parents themselves offer these particular words of advice to others:

- Make quality family time.

- Give siblings a chance to talk things through honestly.

- Involve the siblings in decision making.

- Don't hide the autism spectrum difficulties away.

- Don't suppress your own feelings.

- Allow negative feelings too.

- Set aside time for siblings.

- If possible, try not to split up too much as a family.

- Plan ahead for positive events to look forward to.

- Don't be afraid of getting help or respite.

- Link up with other families to share the burden.

- Try to seek help before things become too tough.

CONFLICT WITH PROFESSIONALS

One of the most difficult aspects of having a child with PDA is the variation in diagnosis of the condition itself and the implications and repercussions that this may have. Parents who suspect their child has PDA, perhaps after it has been mentioned to them or after they have come across literature or information on the internet, frequently come across responses which make getting an appropriate diagnosis very difficult and can bring them into conflict with their professionals. Professionals may not have heard about PDA or may have little understanding of the condition. They might be reluctant to give a diagnosis of PDA because it isn't a term used in the diagnostic manuals, or they may interpret the child's behaviour and needs in a different way. One parent on the PDA Contact Group forum writes:

…two paediatricians in a row more or less made out it was all down to my bad parenting. Luckily they kept moving on and the third paediatrician diagnosed PDA – I had never heard of it. Unfortunately she promptly retired. Round here PDA is considered a 'contentious' diagnosis – they don't dismiss it outright but I am left in no doubt that the authorities will refuse to acknowledge it if they feel like it. Luckily we then went to CAMHS, who were also dismissive at first, but they did indeed diagnose our daughter as having 'ASD with PDA'.

For some parents, they may have had an indication that their child is on the autism spectrum, but they realise the diagnosis isn't a 'good fit'. Some may have been told that their child has 'atypical autism', but many feel that to be told their child is atypical of a condition is unhelpful. A number of voluntary groups, including the National Autistic Society and NORSACA, provide parent support and advice lines for families with a child on the autism spectrum. One senior social care professional involved with such a service told us of her experience of the increasing number of parents of PDA that are contacting them:

Often when I first talk with parents it is with a sense of relief. Parents have been desperate to talk to someone who has some knowledge and understanding of PDA, something that may not have been accessible to them locally. They are relieved that there may be apparent explanations for the day-to-day issues that they have been struggling with, with their youngster's behaviour. By this stage it is common that their child may no longer be within the education system or is enmeshed in a series of fixed period exclusions. The next step for them is then convincing a paediatrician that this would be worthwhile investigating; often at this point an exchange of information is made so that they can pass on information about PDA to the relevant staff. While clinical staff are now familiar with autistic spectrum conditions; many will not have the same knowledge or awareness of PDA. I do alert parents that this is likely to be the start of a long journey, not least 'winning' over sceptical or resistant professionals along the way.

Many parents, already dealing with the practical and emotional issues that have just been described, find themselves having to convince and 'do battle' with the professionals who should be supporting them. For some, their experience can be especially harrowing if their child's behaviour is seen as a reflection of their parenting skills. The following excerpt from a posting on the PDA Contact Group forum, which sadly is not an uncommon one, is from a parent of a child who was later diagnosed with PDA.

Vicky was first highlighted as having problems when she was four. At first I thought it was learnt behaviour from her older brother who has Asperger's, but over time I came to realise that the behaviour was actually part of her nature not her nurture.

Initially, it was suggested that Vicky was suffering from Attachment Disorder and both she and I underwent counselling to help 'repair' our relationship. This was a very difficult time, as to be told that your daughter does not have the ability to form healthy attachments due to your actions is very hard to hear. My husband and I had just separated and this basically supported his belief that I was too soft. Once the sessions ended we were literally discharged and left on our own. By this time we were in our third primary school who were very supportive but conscious of their limitations. Vicky managed to gain funding through the LEA, citing behaviour difficulties as the reason. I accepted this was a means to an end but felt that she was branded 'the naughty girl' when this wasn't the case.

Eventually I rang up the hospital in tears and begged for further help. We had a total of four appointments and then the psychologist suggested that PDA was a possibility and that he would take it to the Special Needs Panel for discussion. Things went from bad to worse…! The paediatrician in charge did not recognise PDA and refused to acknowledge that Vicky had a condition that was part of

ASD. In utter frustration I requested a second opinion at another Children's Hospital, where we met Dr G and her team. At the end of the assessment their findings were discussed with me. When they said that in their opinion Vicky had ASD with a PDA profile I could have cried. I asked if there could be any doubt, any grey area, but they confirmed that in their opinion she fitted all the criteria and required support and help from my local PCT.

After four years of battling with local education authorities and health authorities I have won and my daughter has an appropriate diagnosis. I feel vindicated!

As a parent I have had my parenting skills questioned, my marriage has failed and I have doubted myself to the point where I began to think I wanted my daughter to be ill so was looking for symptoms…(dark times) but now – a light is shining. I feel as though a huge weight has been lifted and I wanted others out there to know that – it may be hard and you may question your ability and sanity but don't. I can now hold my head up and say – I am not a bad parent but the loving parent of a child with PDA!

Slowly recognition and understanding of PDA is improving, and this will gradually lead to more consistent support for families. The key for parents is unlocking the door to understanding, learning and actively engaging with the way in which PDA affects their child and the adjustments and strategies that they can put in place to help them.

It is very frustrating when you know something is wrong but have no diagnosis. Personally, I have always felt that a diagnosis is not a label; it is a signpost to how to provide the best and most suitable interventions possible. (Parent, PDA Contact Group)

CHILDREN WITH PDA GROWING UP

Moving from childhood into adulthood can be a difficult time of life for anyone, and it is no surprise that the same problems will be evident for the individual with PDA too. Coupled with a need for control and high anxiety, this time of life can prove a huge challenge for the young person with PDA and their parents. There are many aspects of a teenager's life which are altering: physical changes happening at puberty; the development of sexuality; increasing self-awareness; transition into secondary school;

increased independence; risk-taking and legal responsibilities. There will be some things that become easier, while other new challenges emerge. In some ways, the extent of the problems may be related to how independent the child or young person is. Along with an ability to become more independent comes an increased need to judge taking risks and to manage their own behaviour. The less able young person with PDA may, in many respects, pose far less risk and worry to their parents. What is more, help and support is usually more forthcoming from other agencies when a child or young person's difficulties are more obvious. During teenage years, a young person's relationships with their peers can become more important to them than their relationships with their family. This can bring additional strain on families living with a child with PDA, and can have implications for guiding that young person to make decisions in their own right, without becoming socially vulnerable or placing themselves in high-risk situations. Balancing independence with risk is an issue for all parents of course, but it is a much more delicate balance for young people with PDA, and is one with potentially more explosive consequences.

Puberty, with its bodily changes, is a time of life that many parents dread, regardless of their child's needs. Parents of children with PDA will worry about the effect that hormones will have on their child's already unpredictable mood swings, and in particular whether they will be able to handle them. Some parents may be in fear of their child being able to overpower them physically. Puberty has different effects on different children, and sometimes, parents' fears never come to fruition. Some children do become more physically challenging though, and this is why earlier diagnosis is valuable to be able to work with children to provide more helpful ways they can deal with their anger and frustration. Issues regarding children's self-awareness, and developing ways for them to manage their own emotional regulation are detailed in Chapter 5.

Parents of girls with PDA will have particular worries about their daughters starting menstruation and how their child will manage with the practicalities on a monthly basis. Although many parents have described their children as adapting well to it, one mother describes her daughter's experience:

I'd prepared Emma for her first period, and she knew what to expect (as best you can). The day she started her period, Emma cried and said it hurt. She wouldn't have a water bottle or take any pain killer. It was hard, but in the end I had to take the line 'this will help, but if you won't take the help you have to suffer the pain', to be around, but to leave her to it.

The next three days, she spent about 20 out of 24 hours just sat on the toilet, waiting for the bleeding to stop – like a three day meltdown, where you couldn't talk any sense to her, Once it was over, we talked about how she could [deal with a period] differently. Since then she's been fine – a 'normal' teenager, a bit moody beforehand, but copes well – she just gets on with it.

Parents of adolescents of either gender may find that having regular baths or showers becomes more of a priority at this age. This is where, of course, it can be helpful to have developed some standards below which the child will not be able to fall without being challenged, alongside some methods for supporting co-operation with personal hygiene, in the earlier years. Even if this has been done, there may be increased priority placed on this issue during puberty, which may or may not bring with it increased conflict. Some of the strategies which may be useful in this respect will be variations on those outlined earlier for dealing with bedtime. These will include giving the young person choices where possible, within agreed limits; such as, the requirement for a full body wash at least every other day, which could be a shower or bath; a choice of which toiletries to use; choosing which part of the day suits best.

Sometimes children with PDA display *sexualised behaviours* or use sexual language that they may have learnt from a variety of sources. Children may use strong language, and may incorporate it within personal comments directed towards individuals. Some children and young people may use behaviours such as pulling down their pants, or trying to touch other people inappropriately. Behaving like this can have a significant impact on a child's surroundings, and on the people they are with. Children on the autism spectrum may also develop inappropriate behaviours of this kind, and may also come to understand that they can use them to influence other people's *behaviour*, but they are not necessarily aware that they can be used in a way that has an impact on other people's *social or emotional responses*. Often this intention to shock, distract or disrupt, by using behaviours which are very hard for most people to ignore, explains their appeal to children with PDA. These behaviours may also reflect issues related to mimicry and role play, and certainly are among the most powerful distraction strategies available to adolescents.

Such behaviours can create tension within a family, particularly where a younger sibling may be hearing language, or witnessing behaviours, which are not in their best interests. Whatever the explanation for these behaviours, managing them can present a considerable challenge, as can ensuring that the young people themselves do not become vulnerable. Equally, it cannot be overlooked that there are occasions when this sort of behaviour is interpreted by adults as being suggestive of potential concerns regarding child protection. Whereas professional agencies, of course, have a duty to take issues such as this seriously, at the same time it can be hard for them to recognise the nature of this behaviour in a child who has apparent verbal and interpersonal skills at one level, yet has difficulties in social understanding as well as in linking their actions to consequences, as is seen in PDA, at another level. Unfortunately that can mean that complex and unnecessarily distressing situations arise from time to time, which again underlines the need for better and earlier identification, and knowledge, of development and awareness in children with PDA.

THE PDA CONTACT GROUP

The PDA Contact Group (www.pdacontact.org.uk) is part of Contact a Family, a national organisation in the UK which helps parents of children with the same diagnoses to get in touch with others in their immediate area. The group was started in 1997 by parents of children with PDA. Since then, it has expanded to include many members worldwide, some of which have started their own local support groups. In 2001 an online forum was set up. Many parental comments within this book have been taken from the PDA Contact Group online forum, where parents have found help and support from each other. Although much of the support is web-based, joining the group enables parents to share techniques and coping strategies with each other and contact others in the same area as themselves, dealing with similar issues. The website is a valuable resource for parents and professionals.

The main aims of the PDA Contact Group are to enable support and increase the general awareness of PDA. It produces advice and leaflets for parents and teachers distributing them to organisations in the UK and around the world. Parents on the forum often express great relief to have found a community that understands the extreme difficulties their family is going through. For those parents, an online support group is invaluable, especially if they are unable to get out in the evenings because it may be hard for them to find childcare.

I always enjoy reading new members' postings. It so reminds me of my first posting and the tears of relief that someone else understood what life was like!! There is always plenty of advice to be had and I know I echo many of us when I say it can be a life saver sometimes! (Parent, PDA Contact Group)

A final message from the contact group:

Count the times you avert disaster and avoid a difficulty, rather than the times you fail. Pat yourself on the back for the better days and don't be too disheartened by the ones that go wrong. Good and bad is not a reflection on your general parenting skills, but a reflection of the complexity of your child's problems.

Chapter 4

PROVIDING THE BEST EDUCATION FOR A CHILD WITH PDA

INTRODUCTION

In broad terms, education is a process by which children are enabled to develop the skills, knowledge and understanding that will enable their full participation in society. Children with PDA have exactly the same entitlement to this as any other children. Ensuring appropriate educational provision is made for a pupil with PDA means tailoring the curriculum, approach and support that is required to the child's individual needs. PDA, like autism, is a 'dimensional' condition, which means that it affects individual children to different extents. It also interacts with other factors in the child's development, as well as their personality and unique circumstances. It is almost always the case, though, that the child's demand avoidance will cause him to function below his potential for much of the time.

Children with PDA may be catered for in the full range of educational placements that are available: mainstream, special or specialist schools, such as those designated for children with ASD. Some children will have been excluded from school after a history of educational failure. On the one hand, there are some children who seem to have learnt that keeping a low profile can reduce pressure and they are relatively compliant at school (usually, though, at the expense of more difficult and challenging behaviour at home). On the other hand, there are those where school provision has broken down altogether and the child receives varying levels and types of individualised support packages from their families and professional agencies. Sadly, it is not uncommon for children with PDA to be placed in a series of schools, as one placement after another breaks down. Key issues for almost any school placement will include how to create an environment for the child in which:

- access to learning opportunities is maximised

- anxiety and any resulting behaviour problems are minimised

- positive peer relationships are supported.

The Elizabeth Newson Centre is often contacted for advice about the most appropriate type of placement for children with PDA, and this is nearly always impossible to answer briefly. It is usually the character and personality of the prospective school that determines its success, rather than any particular 'designation' (for example mainstream or special, day or residential). A genuine commitment to inclusion, strong support from the head teacher and leadership team together with a positive, creative, flexible and adaptable outlook are critical. A commitment to work with the child's family in a supportive and open partnership is also vital.

A lot of material produced for parents of children with special educational needs (SEN) is equally relevant to parents of children with PDA. Much of the information about choosing an appropriate school is produced by local authorities or voluntary organisations and is updated as policies and resources change or develop. There is, though, a very wide variation in the quality of advice that is produced, and many parents report that they do not receive sufficient information or support in making an informed school choice. If parents feel that the information they are being given about educational provision is inadequate, a useful resource, as a starting point, is the local Parent Partnership Service (PPS). This is a statutory service set up to be at 'arm's length' from the local authority (www.parentpartnership. org.uk).

Other material and resources are published nationally by government departments, national charities or legal advice organisations. A list of some of these contacts is published at the back of this book. A particularly useful document in relation to children with autism spectrum disorders is the Autism Education Trust review *Educational Provision for Children and Young People on the Autism Spectrum Living in England* (2008). As well as the full report there are two summary reports; one for parents and carers and another for professionals and providers of services.

A CONTINUUM OF PROVISION FOR A CONTINUUM OF NEED

Over the past two decades the notion of inclusion has been at the heart of education policy. It has been a priority to include pupils with special educational needs in mainstream schools where possible, taking into account the extent of the child's needs and parental wishes. The SEN Code of Practice (DfES 2001) has as one of its fundamental principles that the special educational needs of children will normally be met in mainstream schools or settings.

There has been continuing debate over the meaning of the term 'inclusion' and, in particular, how this differs from 'integration' (which can simply refer to the location in which education takes place, rather than a process of full involvement). The Autism Education Trust's (2008, p.20) report referred to above gives its own definition of what inclusion should mean to a school:

> ...inclusion is the process of including and educating a child within a school (mainstream or special), where the school is able to recognise and assess the pupil's particular needs and is willing and able to be flexible in how the curriculum is delivered and to adapt the routines and physical environment the pupil is expected to operate within. Particular attention is given to the relationships the pupil is enabled to develop with other pupils...both within and outside the school, and the potential benefits to other pupils and staff.

The vast majority of educational provision in England is funded by local authorities and takes place either in schools and services provided by authorities themselves, or in the private, voluntary and independent sectors and funded by the local authority. Provision for children with SEN, including those with PDA, will include:

- mainstream schools in which provision may or may not be enhanced by additional adult support or involvement from specialist outreach services

- special schools or units for children with a range of SEN, again with or without additional support

- schools, units or enhanced resource classes specifically for children on the autism spectrum

- schools or other provision for children with other designated SEN (e.g. social, emotional and behavioural difficulties)

- special individual programmes for children who do not attend school.

There is little research evidence to suggest what the relative benefits of each type of placement are and which children benefit most from specialist or mainstream provision. It is also, of course, the case that the quality of practice in schools within the same 'category' varies enormously according to, for example, the experience and skills of the staff. This makes generalisations about types of placement very difficult. In addition to the characteristics and experiences of the child, many factors will influence decisions about what placement is made and how successful it is. These include the experience and attitudes of school staff, the provision that is available in a particular area, parents' views and also those of the pupil if they can obtained.

While it is entirely appropriate that such a range of provision exists, given that children with PDA have different levels of need and ability, it is also the case that different local authorities arrange their provision in different ways. This is true both in terms of the placements they provide and those they agree to fund externally. This variation in provision often leads parents to feel that the choices they may be offered are guided more by the resources that are available than by a genuine assessment of their child's individual needs. It can also result in parental confusion or anger when they are not able to access services that they would like in their own local area. In an ideal situation the decision about where a child is placed within this continuum of provision would reflect an accurate assessment and shared understanding of the extent of a child's needs at a particular time and stage in their development.

Evidence suggests that the experience parents of children with special educational needs have of the education system is extremely varied. Brian Lamb, who oversaw the inquiry into special educational needs and parental confidence, opened his report (Lamb 2009) by saying that he had met 'some of the happiest parents in the country and some of the angriest'. Seen from the perspective of a voluntary organisation and parent support group it would seem to be the case that many more parents of children with PDA fall into the latter group than the former. Most will have experienced delay and frustration in reaching a diagnosis that makes sense of their child and then have similar problems ensuring their child's needs are more widely understood and adequately met.

Mainstream schools

Almost all children with PDA will start their education in a mainstream setting and it is unlikely at this stage that their special educational needs will have been recognised. It is even less likely that a diagnosis of PDA will have been given. Central to the Code of Practice is the idea of a 'graduated response', whereby schools and settings should continually assess and monitor the child's progress. This should then lead to them making adjustments by using all the available resources in the school before calling upon specialist expertise from outside. It is as part of this process that the need for external advice, additional support, a statutory assessment or change of school placement may be raised according to the views of parents, the school and local authority. For a school-aged child this process involves three stages. School Action (where the school makes adaptations without recourse to external agencies), School Action Plus (where external agencies such as the educational psychology service become involved) and Statement of Special Educational Needs (which is discussed in more detail in a later section).

Continuing in *mainstream provision* clearly has some potential advantages in that the child remains within his local community, has access to a wide ranging curriculum together with opportunities for social interaction and the development of social relationships with typically developing peers. However, for the majority of children with PDA, the school is likely to have to make significant adjustments in many areas to ensure the child's needs are adequately met. If the principles and guidelines outlined in Chapter 2 are to be embraced, this has implications for staff training and attitudes, as well as those that may relate to the environment and additional resources. The needs of children with PDA are often unrecognised and misunderstood in ways that have already been described, which means that attitudes and expectations of staff in any school are central. In some mainstream schools, pupils have simply been expected to fit in to existing routines and structures without any adaptation. For some children, when this is insisted on, it can have distressing effects for all concerned.

The Autism Education Trust (2008, p.20) report goes on to quote Rita Jordan (Professor of Autism Studies, Birmingham University):

> A child with a visual impairment would not be placed in a school without low vision aids and mobility training…yet a pupil on the autism spectrum is often expected to manage in school without these equivalent supports and be expected to be able to act and respond as other typical children.

Some mainstream schools, though, especially during the primary phase, are able to make these necessary adjustments and are tenacious in their commitment to meeting the child's needs in a fully inclusive fashion. This becomes much more difficult, though, at secondary level, due to the sheer number of pupils and the way in which the curriculum and teaching and learning are organised.

Ben's mum provided this account of his progress within *mainstream provision*:

As Ben progressed through nursery school, it became apparent he would need additional support. While in reception at a supportive school, without any specific one-to-one support, there were numerous occasions when he would hit out, spit or throw things. These situations usually happened when other children got in Ben's way, interrupted his games or during unstructured times, such as playtime. Ben could interact sometimes, if the game or situation was on his terms and could appear 'rude' to adults as he was very direct asking questions like 'Why do you look like that?'.

Between the ages of four and five, Ben would often exhibit anxious, unpredictable behaviour, such as running out of the classroom, throwing bricks or sand in the air or suddenly deciding 'I need to go', or 'I need juice', which would require immediate action from the adult there. During interactions with teachers or teaching staff, Ben was often observed changing the subject when asked to complete a task, or seeming to have a very poor attention span. He was often completely uninterested in group activities and needed constant monitoring for his own safety and that of others. Other parents complained that he had 'hurt' their child, and there were concerns about health and safety and his development if he didn't receive more one-to-one support.

Once in Year 1 (ages 5–6), Ben was granted a full-time one-to-one support. The transformation began slowly, but within a year he became a very different boy. He became calmer, stopped hitting and hurting at school, and started to form several relationships with trusted peers. His teaching assistant, a very experienced support worker, created a 'quiet' room where Ben would work and produced individualised learning aids to help him. So, for example, if all the class were asked to use their imaginations to write a story, his teaching assistant might use some props to prompt Ben's imagination and then she would begin by writing the story down on a whiteboard. Ben would then be encouraged to take part. His areas of expertise were maths and numbers. A home/school diary was created to 'rate' how Ben was achieving throughout school and this was carefully managed to boost Ben's confidence, backed up by regular after-school treats to places he enjoyed, such as an indoor play centre, or a garden centre to see the fountains. Ben's anxiety gradually decreased as he became more confident with his teaching assistant. She says she worked as a 'facilitator', helping Ben to build friendships, understand the unwritten rules of the playground and learn what was appropriate. Ben's demand avoidance eased as staff worked pragmatically to make the classroom and the pressures easier on him. Fears about exclusion eased and school became a very positive experience, for the whole family.

Ben is now eight years old and is in Year 4. He still has full-time one-to-one support, which is split between two experienced, flexible and caring professionals. He is a very different boy who is achieving well in many areas, has several close friends at school and is confident. His reliance on his support staff has decreased, but there are still times when he needs clarification about situations or is anxious. Any anti-social behaviour is greatly reduced; in fact, Ben is a very caring, conscientious boy who looks after his younger brother and prides himself on 'being kind'. Socially he is still underdeveloped and often seems 'switched' off, a term to describe when he doesn't appear to be able to focus or concentrate. This may be because of the high levels of concentration he requires to get through the day and Ben seems to enjoy having down time, playing computer games, although with boundaries (a short session timed with a digital timer).

We believe that by finding two schools that were flexible, understanding and willing to work with us and Ben, means that he is flourishing. Their approach and having skilled additional support have helped to shape Ben's view of the world positively.

Increasingly local authorities are providing *units*, or specific classes, *within mainstream schools* that have been specifically set up for pupils on the autism spectrum. These may be in schools that have been designated as having a focus on children on the spectrum beyond the school's usual catchment area. This provision might be organised in different ways, such as a designated base but with pupils included for part of their time in classes within the main part of the school.

Mikey's mum describes how his needs were met in an *integrated resource within a mainstream school*:

We made the decision to change Mikey to an integrated resource (IR) within a mainstream school after he had been excluded from one mainstream very early on and only went part time to the second mainstream. At the first school they had never seen a child behave like Mikey before. They described him as manipulative and felt unable to support him at all without 1:1 support. We kept having to take him home at 10 or 11 every morning and he had several fixed-term exclusions when his behaviour was unmanageable and he'd bitten one of the teaching assistants. At the second mainstream school, while they were much more sympathetic and eager to try many different things to help, they took nearly a year to get him in full time and even then he wasn't really reaching his potential as they were only just managing his behaviour.

The integrated resource is situated right in the centre of the school. Each child within the resource has a designated member of staff, although they are flexible about this if the child is able to tolerate it. Each child attempts to be in the mainstream class, with their support, for the whole morning and then is timetabled to be in the resource for the afternoon, where small group teaching of social skills and peer group teaching takes place. There is a sensory room, which is timetabled into their week, and a quiet room, which is where the child can go in times of great stress or meltdown – a safe space. Each child has a detailed Individual Educational Plan and each timetable is tailored to each particular child.

When Mikey first started at the resource he was in the mainstream part of the school very little and was in the quiet room quite a lot. But the school coped, developed plans, and they were not looking to me to provide all the answers either. Gradually, with the ingenuity and flexibility of both the support staff and the teachers, Mikey gradually became more able to be involved in the mainstream classes. When I look back at the amount of work he did in the first year there, as compared to the last year at his old school, I am amazed at the difference. Each year he has made incredible progress. Now with the help of a scribe and planned breaks he took some mock SATs and gained results equivalent to, and greater than, some of his peers. He has made good friendships. He also went on a week's residential trip, which I had great reservations about, but he managed it with the right planning and support in place. He was very proud of himself for that and it gave his self-esteem a massive boost. He has had, essentially, the same support teacher for three years now, although in the last year he has had different support for different lessons – finding the most appropriate person for different subjects. There are a couple of other children who have PDA there and the staff have taken on board the handling guidelines and have attended training. The school has a very inclusive and flexible attitude and the head teacher has a strong influence in this. Mikey has even said he enjoys school, which after the very rocky start he had to his education was a milestone for us. Now we just have to hope our choice for secondary will match the success we have had at the IR.

Special or specialist schools

Special or *specialist provision* will be considered by many parents, particularly if they have already had a negative experience within mainstream. They may be attracted by the smaller class sizes, easier access to supporting therapies, more extensive experience in working with children on the autism spectrum and those with challenging behaviour, together with the greater emphasis that is usually given to the curriculum on personal and social development.

Neesha and her parents experienced increasing difficulties in a series of mainstream schools and the situation improved significantly for them when she transferred to a *specialist school for children with ASDs* after a very carefully planned transition.

Neesha was excluded from her first mainstream school in Year 2 (ages 6–7). She then joined her second mainstream school in the spring of her Year 3, having had a period of three months out of school. The second school made efforts to help her settle in, to participate in classroom activities, and provided some additional teaching assistant support time. However, by the time she was in her second term of Year 5 (ages 9–10), difficulties were becoming more frequent and enduring. Getting to school on time in the mornings was complicated and stressful for her and her parents; she would regularly abscond from school if she was upset; she was uncomfortable when being taught with the rest of the class, yet felt excluded and targeted if she was withdrawn for 1:1 sessions. Instances of challenging behaviour increased, which at times led to her parents being contacted to come to take her home. She was spending less and less time at school and when she was there, she was not often engaged in learning opportunities. She was becoming more socially isolated and her self-esteem was deteriorating. At the start of Year 6 (ages 10–11), she was attending school for mornings only, she was either taking herself home or parents were being asked to collect her on a frequent basis and she was not spending time in class with her peer group at all. Staff and parents felt that the school was no longer able to meet her needs.

Neesha joined a specialist school situated some distance away from her home halfway through Year 6. Although there were some issues to balance between getting the appropriate setting and staff expertise and finding an appropriate peer group, it was felt that a specialist school was the most beneficial placement for her at this time. A careful package was devised in collaboration with her parents to ease her transition in a positive and motivating way. Initially, her class teacher made a series of short visits to her at home in order to build a relationship with Neesha. These visits were sociable and flexible and were usually spent playing games or chatting. In between these visits, Neesha made some visits to her new school, after the end of the school day so that she could explore the school environment without other pupils being there. After a period of three weeks, Neesha began to come to school on a daily basis. Initially this meant arriving half an hour after other pupils in order to miss the hustle and bustle of the start of the school day, and staying just for the morning. She was taught in a separate classroom with two members of rotated staff who she knew the best at this stage, and spent her time largely on activities and games which she found motivating. School staff met briefly, but daily, to evaluate progress and were in regular contact with Neesha's parents. Together they decided when to increase the time she spent at school, how to extend the activities she did while there and how to include her for short periods in classroom-based activities alongside other pupils. For example, she was encouraged to stay at school for lunch by having a cookery session at 11.30 during which she made some lunch for herself and her teacher. These decisions were taken slowly and with careful consideration. At the end of a period of three months (one school term) she was integrated into a small class group and was attending full time.

At a review meeting after her first term at the specialist school her parents wrote, 'She is finally finding school a rewarding experience. Her self-esteem and confidence are building steadily and she is generally calmer. She feels that she has friends at school and is actually making progress in her work. She fits in somewhere for the first time in her life. I don't think we could have made a better choice for her.'

In some special schools, though, staff expectations and attitudes may still be a problem and there can be disadvantages in relation to the suitability of the peer group and ensuring the provision of a sufficiently challenging curriculum. The wider catchment areas served by special schools may also reduce opportunities outside of school for some pupils.

The nature of the peer group is an especially important consideration and will obviously depend on the particular population of the special school. Partly because special schools are relatively small, there can also be considerable variation between different year groups. There are often specific issues for girls, with a much higher proportion of boys within special schools, particularly those for children on the autism spectrum. The response of children with PDA to other children within special schools is varied and, in some individual cases, surprising. Some children find it very hard to identify with those who have significant learning difficulties, which can have a negative effect on their self-esteem and, at times, lead to them being unkind to other children. Other children with PDA seem to react in a very different way, perhaps feeling less pressured to compete with their peers and take on supportive and caring roles. This issue is discussed further in the later section on social opportunities and supporting positive relationships.

From our own experience it has not always been easy to predict which child will react in a certain way to the other pupils in a prospective school, and the pupil's own views and attitudes about this, and other factors, have a very important role to play in decisions about school choice.

In the end choosing and making the most suitable provision for an individual child with PDA most often represents something of a compromise. For example, one school may have better staffing levels and have had experience of children with PDA but be less well equipped to provide for a child's curriculum requirements. Another may seem to be able to provide access to a more appropriate curriculum and peer group, but have less experience dealing with some of the behavioural challenges that a child with PDA may present. As was pointed out in the introduction to this chapter, it is likely to be the character and ethos of a prospective school which is most likely to influence its success. In making their choice of school, parents need to make their own judgements about this and consider a number of factors which make up provision, accepting that they may need to compromise on some of these. When thinking about some of the factors that a school might seem to have difficulty in providing for a child, it is important to consider whether this can be found in any other way. For example, if a special school doesn't seem to provide sufficient opportunities for social interaction with pupils who have similar communication levels, can this be provided through inclusion opportunities within a school with which it has links? Or in the case of a unit or enhanced resource, can these opportunities be provided for in the main part of the school? If a mainstream school has little experience of working with children with PDA, does it have access to outreach support and advice?

In trying to make a judgement and choice between schools, some of the key variables that need to be considered might include those listed in the box opposite.

The next section considers these factors in more detail, and a list of questions for parents to ask when visiting a school can be found at the end of the chapter.

FACTORS TO TAKE INTO ACCOUNT WHEN MAKING DECISIONS ABOUT SCHOOLS

- Characteristics of the head and staff (e.g. flexibility, openness, commitment to inclusion).

- Understanding, expertise and experience of the staff in relation to children with PDA/ASD.

- Size of class groups. Does this change across the school?

- Ratio of staff to pupils in different class groups.

- Amount of individual support that might be available.

- Access to outside specialist advice (e.g. outreach services).

- Availability of therapy and other resources.

- Characteristics of the peer group. How will this impact on the child with PDA?

- Involvement and support offered to parents and families.

- Appropriateness of the curriculum to the child's learning needs.

- Flexibility in differentiating the curriculum for individual needs.

- The school's policy and approach to managing challenging behaviour.

- The school's SEN and exclusion policy.

WHAT MAKES A GOOD SCHOOL FOR CHILDREN WITH PDA?

School management and whole-school approach

Crucial to the successful placement of a child with PDA, in any school, is the attitude and approach of the senior management or leadership team. While adults working in classrooms need to be flexible, indirect and child-centred, this is not sufficient to maintain a successful placement. The management team needs to equally flexible and committed to the inclusion of the child with PDA within their school community. This flexibility in leadership is necessary for all staff to feel confident and supported in ensuring that there is sufficient differentiation and personalisation in the curriculum offered and in the way in which it is delivered.

For some children, the level of differentiation required can be exceptional. There are times when this might be comparatively easily managed by the staff within the child's class group. It may, though, be less easily achieved throughout the school as a whole. Frequently, other staff may find it harder to understand, or accept, some of the differences in the way the individual child is managed. This could be because they haven't been given sufficient information, because they are worried about the impact of the child on others in the school or feel that there is a measure of 'unfairness' in treating one child so differently. The potential for these sorts of conflicts to arise underlines the need for good communication systems and whole-school training opportunities.

Individual staff characteristics

In Chapter 2 the transactional (or two-way) nature of interactions was emphasised. Adults working with children with PDA need to reflect on their own contribution to the process of teaching and learning as much as the child's. Their own understanding of PDA, as well as their attitudes and beliefs, underpins the effectiveness of their interactions. Adults working with children with PDA need to be very flexible in their approach and be able to deliver a creative, non-directive teaching style for much of the time. At the same time, though, they need to be confident, calm and quietly insistent when enforcing necessary boundaries. They need to be able to de-personalise difficult behaviour and be prepared to 'wipe the slate clean' as often as is needed. As well as this, they should be reflective, a good listener and team member. Maintaining these characteristics and sustaining positive interactions is not straightforward, and a later section considers some of the support needs of staff.

Curriculum

In schools in England and Wales, since the creation of the National Curriculum in 1988, there has been an emphasis on the notion of entitlement: that all children are entitled to the same range of educational opportunities. Alongside this aspiration it was emphasised that the curriculum should be *broad* (giving pupils a wide range of experience), *balanced* (ensuring a balanced distribution of this experience), *differentiated* (according to the individual needs of a pupil) and *relevant* (to their particular circumstances). Given that a curriculum should provide experiences that meet *all* of a child's educational needs, the National Curriculum can only be part of the curriculum offered to a child. The curriculum provided for a child with PDA is likely to need significant differentiation. The child will need much greater emphasis placed on personal and social education to focus on areas such as independence and self-awareness. It is also likely to be the case that differentiation will be needed to ensure that teaching can build on a child's strengths and interests, even if these might seem rather unusual. Sometimes children with PDA will respond well to a cross-curricular approach, whereby a topic is based around a particular interest and incorporates other areas of the curriculum in such a way that disguises subjects that the child might be more resistant to.

Duncan (aged 11), mentioned in earlier examples, attended a specialist school, following his previous mainstream placement becoming unsuitable and unsustainable. By the time his mainstream placement was breaking down in Year 4 (ages 8–9), he was being taught in a separate room and was not often at school for whole days, usually due to incidents of challenging behaviour. He was lacking in self-confidence, socially isolated and very anxious about demands being made of him. Following a period of careful transition to the specialist school, staff used his personal interests to get him engaged in learning in a motivated and meaningful way.

In the example given on pp.59–60 it was described how staff understood that he was highly resistant to completing any task that he perceived as 'set school work'. He also avoided tasks which involved writing or working with a group of peers. He was, however, naturally very inquiring and enjoyed discussing ideas. He became interested in the *Horrid History* series of books and television programmes, especially in the Romans. He particularly liked to find out gruesome facts about how they lived and died, what they ate, their standards of hygiene, and their table manners. Within the context of relationships of trust which staff had built with Duncan, he was offered a series of 'missions and challenges' (rather than 'school work') which were based on this interest. Staff let him lead the topic, sensitively facilitating his research or recording, in order to create a unit of cross-curricular work which spanned most of a school term. He completed maths activities based around developing telling the time using a sundial. He got involved in literacy and food technology work by researching and cooking Roman recipes, which he then 'dared' staff to taste and grade on a score chart. He did some work in social history by investigating Roman life and class structure. He carried out geographic and scientific research as well as experiments based around the theme of volcanoes. He produced art work using mosaic designs.

Throughout these activities there was a low-key attitude, of doing things for the sake of fun not for curriculum learning. Duncan felt that he was able to guide the line of research and any ensuing projects. The role of staff was sensitively to ease his path through various investigations, taking care to keep the balance between encouraging him to stay motivated and on task on the one hand (often by doing the least favoured part of the work such as writing), while trying to stretch his co-operation and knowledge on the other.

Some mainstream schools find it harder than others to individualise a child's learning experiences, or to give a child opportunities outside the general curricular needs of the other children. This is an area where flexibility and commitment on the part of the management team is important. On the other hand, some special or specialist schools, especially at secondary level, may find it harder to have subject expertise across the full curriculum. Some may be able to supplement this by providing specialist teachers on a sessional basis or enabling students to access particular areas of the curriculum by providing sessions at other schools or colleges.

Individual Education Plans

At the heart of the process of curriculum differentiation and planning for a child with identified special educational needs is an Individual Education Plan (IEP), which is typically drawn up once a term. This should set out short-term targets, the teaching strategies to be used, the provision that needs to be in place and what outcomes are expected. The plan should be based on an assessment of a child's attainments, progress and needs. In the case of a child with PDA, making an accurate assessment of attainments is particularly complex because of their uneven profile, variability in different settings and tendency to function below their potential much of the time. The process of drawing up the IEP should both include consultation with parents and take account the views of the pupil.

Guidance in the Code of Practice is that that the IEP should record that which is 'additional to or different from' the curriculum which is in place for all pupils. It also suggests that targets focus on three or four individual objectives taken from the key areas of communication, literacy, maths, and behaviour and social skills. Within a good classroom, considerably more targets and strategies will need to be in place, and reflected in an individual programme, tailored for a particular child's needs. It is likely that monitoring progress against these objectives and the strategies used will need to take place frequently. Targets will also need to focus on priority areas, such as social understanding, personal, social and health education (PSHE) and behaviour. The strategies are also likely to comprise the indirect approaches and methods described in Chapter 2.

In the box over the page there are some examples of targets from the individual programmes for pupils at Sutherland House, which illustrate both these curriculum priorities and the use of indirect strategies as a way of working towards the targets.

Emotional well-being and behaviour

As part of the emphasis that needs to be given to PSHE within the curriculum, attention will need to be given to ways of working with and relating to the child that promotes emotional well-being. The significance of this area is increasingly seen as important for all children. This is especially the case for children with any form of autism spectrum disorder, because of the recognition of the prevalence and impact of mental health problems for children and young people with this diagnosis (NAS 2010). This area is considered so important for children with PDA that a separate chapter is devoted to it (see Chapter 5).

Additional support (TAs, therapy, outreach teams)

Most children with PDA, whatever their type of school placement, will require additional support beyond that which is available as part of the

COMMUNICATION

To develop her understanding that other people have different views by playing barrier games such as Guess Who? and Battleships.

To gather views and preferences from other pupils in the class as class representative before group discussion to plan community visits.

To share what she has done at the weekend by playing 20 questions.

To find out what others have done at the weekend by 'interviewing' them using a dictaphone.

LITERACY

To demonstrate her understanding of correct use of punctuation by correcting adult's worksheet which includes deliberate errors.

To create a scrapbook about making jewellery including some written information outlining her recommendations, instructions and preferences (these may be dictated to a member of staff in less tolerant sessions).

MATHS

To indicate her answers to maths tasks by using simple multiple-choice approaches (options are adjusted to stay within tolerance level as well as ability level).

To learn how to use a digital clock by setting cooking times when baking.

BEHAVIOUR AND SOCIAL SKILLS

To design and set out PE apparatus circuit and demonstrate instructions for use in order to help her to participate in PE sessions.

To walk between school buildings independently in her role as 'message monitor' to deliver items or letters in order to increase independence and social problem-solving skills.

To play a favourite game with a less familiar member of staff as an introduction to getting to know them.

typical provision within the classroom. This may be in terms of additional individual hours from a teaching assistant, specialist input from speech and language or occupational therapists or consultancy advice from specialist outreach teams (such as ASD or behavioural support teams). For schools who have less experience of working with children with complex profiles, this advisory role can be critical in highlighting teaching strategies and resources. In the case of individual teaching assistants, the success or otherwise of a particular placement may be largely dependent on the quality of these individual relationships. This can present challenges, both in terms of ensuring that all staff concerned with a child receive appropriate training (which is sometimes less easily available for teaching assistants) and in co-ordinating approaches and strategies. Part of the role of the senior management team in this respect is to try to ensure that there is sufficient time for staff to attend meetings and reviews so that advice can be taken up and that decisions reflect everyone's views and are communicated effectively.

Wider support (home, school, family support, etc.)

Parents should very much be regarded as part of the team when discussing priorities and drawing up plans for their child, but many parents feel that they are not listened to during decision-making processes. Parental confidence in their child's provision is highly influential to its success. Schools need to be imaginative and flexible in the way that they provide opportunities for including parents' views and communicating with them about their child's progress and behaviour in school. As well as parents coming into school for more formal meetings such as annual reviews, other opportunities for communication might include daily home/school diaries, telephone conversations, home visits, opportunities for parents to observe in school and have less formal times when they can meet with staff. Clearly the type and level of contact that suits schools and families best is very individual and requires negotiation and compromise on both parts.

Parents frequently report that what they value most in their contact with schools is a positive attitude towards their child and an open and honest relationship, whereby a school can share their uncertainties as well as their successes. As described at the end of Chapter 2, some children can be quite variable in the way they behave in different settings, and this can be potentially divisive. Some children seem to manage the school day without too many behavioural outbursts but then be more avoidant and controlling at home where their behaviour is much more challenging. Parents in this situation often feel blamed by schools and other professionals and feel that they are being judged and criticised for not being able to enforce boundaries. On the other hand, some children find home life much easier because families are able to be more adaptive and responsive to their needs, and the problems become more apparent in school. Rather than letting this situation be destructive to relationships, it is important to try to understand what it is the child finds easier, or more difficult, in different settings and use this understanding in supportive way.

Children with PDA and their families require a holistic approach that recognises their needs beyond the school day. The research carried out with families of children with an ASD by the Autism Education Trust highlighted the stress that many are under and the factors that make it difficult for children and young people to access activities out of school and in the evening. Schools can play a pivotal role in providing information and support to families on both a practical and emotional level. This might include the direct provision of extended school services and becoming a focus for multi-agency collaboration, which might involve supporting families in accessing short-break facilities, access to playschemes, parent support groups or opportunities for befriending. This co-ordinated approach is likely to achieve better outcomes for both children and families.

Taking account of the views of the child or young person

Over recent years, increasing emphasis has been given to the need for schools to consider ways in which the voice of the child or young person can be better heard in the planning and delivery of services. In the UK this is emphasised in *Working Together: Listening to the Voices of Children and Young People* (DCSF 2008). At the school level this should include participation in annual reviews, involvement of the child in setting aims and targets and evaluating their learning opportunities. Of course, this can be challenging for children with complex communication difficulties who may not have the language necessary to articulate more complex thoughts.

For the child or young person with PDA, issues of co-operation and trust are also factors. Chapter 5 gives many examples of strategies and techniques that can be used to support the child's communication, problem-solving skills and ability to judge appropriate assertiveness. A commitment to including children with PDA in this way underlines the importance of the regular tutorial sessions described. This means that children get used to having the sort of dialogue with a trusted member of staff that promotes their capacity to articulate their views and preferences.

Some young people may find joining a meeting involving a number of professionals too intimidating, even though they might have a clear idea of what they want to express. In these situations, work carried out in preparatory sessions might be presented and followed up on their behalf.

SUPPORT NEEDS OF STAFF

However a child with PDA interacts with an adult, the child is only part of that interaction. As we have said, interaction is a transactional process, that is, it is not something delivered 'to' or 'at' a person, but is a two-way exchange. Sustaining positive interactions with children with PDA is not straightforward, and this needs to be recognised. The degree of challenge some youngsters with PDA present can leave adults feeling de-skilled and demoralised. This can apply equally to parents, of course, which is why it is also crucial to work closely with families.

There are a number of reasons why working (or living) with these children requires such stamina:

- Navigating everyday demands positively when you are supporting someone who is prone to unpredictable and even explosive behaviour can be very tiring because it requires you to remain in a state of alertness all the time.

- Being on the receiving end of personal comments, sometimes including insults, is not always easy to overcome.

- At times, balancing the needs of the child with PDA with those of others in the class, particularly if they're vulnerable or their education is being compromised, can be challenging.

- Constantly having to think flexibly and spot potential flashpoints can feel draining – in addition, many usual teaching techniques are not effective so need regular adaptation.

- Reminding yourself that there is often a mismatch between how this child is behaving or what he is saying, and how he is really feeling can be difficult, especially in the heat of the moment.

- Spending time with someone who does not make accommodations for you and your state of mind can be exhausting.

- Staying in role as a 'calm adult' and showing no 'chinks in your armour', even in difficult, situations can be very hard. Sometimes children with PDA will become more anxious and driven to control if they pick up on your uncertainty.

Of course not all of these apply in every case, but many people who work closely with children with PDA will have felt the pressures of some of these factors.

Experience of a range of settings making provision for youngsters with PDA has highlighted a number of key points that school staff should keep in mind to help them to support each other and work effectively:

- *Build up a team* of people who can work together effectively and who can not only understand and support each other but who can also be rotated from time to time to avoid saturation for any one individual (this is of course more difficult for families).

- *Maintain clear direction and leadership* within this team – keep everyone up to date and informed of any new behaviours or decisions, and work towards an improved understanding of PDA.

- Make opportunities to *seek advice* from more experienced staff, receive training and *engage in reflective, collaborative practice*, which will include effective partnership with parents.

- Have *regular, open and honest team meetings* – include a range of adults working with the child and allow people to acknowledge the challenges as well as the achievement.

- In difficult situations, *resist the temptation to 'win'* or have the last word yourself; *slow your decision making* if you feel that you are being out-manoeuvred by the child; and remember to use humour and your relationship with this child to defuse and de-personalise potential flashpoints.

One school as part of its own reflective practice asked staff, through a short survey, about the key features that had helped them work effectively with a number of pupils with PDA. Their responses included:

- Taking time to build relationships of trust with pupils has been invaluable – it's often your best strategy.

- Maintaining a strong ethos of mutual understanding and support, with in-house training, advice and post-incident analysis has been very useful.

- Looking closely at my style has been important, e.g. using non-directive approaches, sense of humour, rising above insults, not backing myself into a corner and regularly reflecting on what I do, how and why.

When they were asked what advice they would give to those who were new to working with children with PDA, they said:

- Remember that 'less is usually more'.

- Reflect on your own input and impact regularly.

- Understand that handing over the balance of power to the child is often the best way to achieve better outcomes for everyone.

- Be non-judgemental, flexible, clear enough to be fair, but unpredictable enough to be interesting.

- Don't be afraid to admit if you are struggling to manage the child – use the support and experience of other staff.

- Prioritise building and maintaining a positive relationship, be prepared to reduce your expectations and take nothing personally.

- Be prepared to start afresh as often as is necessary.

When they were asked to comment on the most enjoyable aspects of working with children with PDA, they said:

- a sense of shared pride and pleasure when something is achieved successfully

- a good sense of humour and appealing personality

- feeling that we can build a meaningful and rewarding relationship

- stimulating socially and challenging professionally

- the additional satisfaction to be had from engaging with a child who is exceptionally hard to engage.

SOCIAL OPPORTUNITIES AND SUPPORTING POSITIVE RELATIONSHIPS

In her original paper on educational and handling guidelines, Elizabeth Newson (1998) put forward the view that a mainstream school is 'appropriate wherever possible' for children with PDA. This was based on the recognition that children with PDA have greater sociability than those with other autism spectrum disorders and that, because they are socially imitative, could benefit from the role-models of typically developing peers. This view has often been questioned by parents whose children may be struggling to receive an appropriate level of education and to cope in this environment. However, as an objective, this must be true for any child with additional needs and the important qualification is that of *wherever possible*. For all the reasons that have already been mentioned, the choice of the most suitable provision and placement is about balancing a whole range of factors.

If we are considering how to promote and maintain positive relationships with other children, it is necessary to look at the impact on both the child with PDA and his classmates. Children with PDA are typically very socially naïve and often have a desire to form friendships and relationships but lack the skills, particularly in negotiation and compromise, to form truly reciprocal relationships. Children with PDA can very easily be 'set up' by other children or become targets for resentment from peers. Their behaviour can also be very hard for other children to make sense of, understand and predict. Other children often find it hard to understand why concessions seem to be made to children with PDA, or they lose tolerance with their controlling behaviour.

On the other hand, peers may well need support to tolerate the disruption that the child with PDA may cause within the classroom. This is especially so for those children with PDA who react to social demands by physically lashing out, shouting or swearing. Some teachers or parents, understandably, have concerns about the impact of this on the learning environment of other children, particularly if the child with PDA is not effectively supported. The school, therefore, has to work proactively both to prevent bullying and teasing of the child with PDA and to support other children in the class so as to minimise any negative impact on their learning. In consultation with the parents of the child with PDA, some form of discussion and preparation is usually helpful; ideally this will be done before the child joins a particular school or class group. The ability to do this, of course, will be dependent upon the identification and diagnosis of an individual child's needs. Preparing other children is best done informally in the same way that might be done in respect of other children with additional needs. This may be done by stories, or other material, that emphasise the uniqueness of each individual child and that describe some of the strengths as well as difficulties that the specific child may have. Later this may lead on to explanations of individual behaviour, such as 'Jamie gets a bit upset when…' and may also include strategies such as 'Jamie finds it easier when we try to do it like this…'.

Explanation of some of the strategies and approaches that staff are using and how the children may themselves respond to certain situations can also be incorporated. In some situations a more formal 'circle of friends' (Newton, Taylor and Wilson 1996) has been found to be particularly helpful in mainstream schools for this sort of preventative work for children with a range of additional needs, including those with an autism spectrum disorder and PDA. The booklet by Julie Davies and Elizabeth Newson (1994) written for the brothers and sisters of children with PDA, can also be adapted as a basis for informing the peer group. Some of the material published to explain autism to brothers and sisters, or other children, can also be useful although may need adapting. The National Autistic Society has a useful list of books and resources on its website and some are referred to on the resource list at the end of this book.

As was mentioned in Chapter 1, children with PDA often have strong fascinations that are of a social nature and that can revolve around specific individuals. The example was given of Adam who became a particular focus for Tim's attention. At its strongest this sort of behaviour can be seen as a form of targeting or 'bullying' of an individual and may require specific, proactive intervention for both of the children involved.

Concerns regarding the child with PDA and their peer group apply not just to those children who are within mainstream provision, though different issues can apply for the child placed in a special or specialist setting. Many children with PDA are placed in special school settings because of the advantages these schools may bring in terms of class sizes and experience in managing challenging behaviours. This may, though, result in the child with PDA being educated alongside children who are less able in terms of curriculum or communication skills and who also have a range of other less typical behaviours. Sometimes this can result in children with PDA finding it hard to see themselves as part of the school population and question why they have been placed there. There may also be issues with them copying some of their peers' less desirable behaviours or even targeting vulnerable pupils. In the same way as with a typically developing peer group, preparation and discussion, both with the individual child with PDA and other pupils in their class or school, is the key to making this work for everyone concerned.

Duncan is an articulate, curious and socially motivated child who is developing an understanding of his own strengths and difficulties. These were highlighted in a new way to him once he moved from a mainstream peer group, to a different range of other peers at the specialist school. Making sense of this was something that his specialist school and his family had anticipated, and they worked closely together to try to explain things to Duncan in a meaningful way while protecting his self-image.

He enjoyed talking about all sorts of 'questions and conundrums', such as:

- What would it be like if everything in the world was made of chocolate?

- What if swearing was no longer offensive or shocking? What would you say when you were really cross?

- What would be a good world record for me to attempt? (It would probably be best to try one that had never been attempted before so that I don't have an existing record to break.)

This led on to include questions such as:

- What if everyone was the same?

- Looked the same?

- Liked the same things?

- Had the same strengths and the same difficulties?

Within the context of answering these questions, he was able to appreciate that it would raise other problems if everyone was indeed too similar. People need to be different in order to push boundaries and to complement each other. The challenge, of course, is finding a way of living alongside other people who are different from you in less compatible ways. Early on he said of some of the other children at the specialist school, 'What am I doing here? These children have special needs! Some of them can't even talk!'

The responses to this type of query required working closely with Duncan's family to make sure that the messages we gave him were consistent. They also required careful pacing regarding how much information to give him at any one point so that he felt listened to and informed, without feeling insecure and confused.

Duncan was able to reflect back on his experience in the mainstream school and consider the differences between himself and his other peers there. He was able to appreciate some of the difficulties he had there about feeling misunderstood and incompatible. He did sometimes feel that he fell somewhere between the two settings though. A while after he had transferred to the specialist school, he commented, 'I'm quite clever really. I could go to a different school, not like this one. I'm not like the others here. I'd like to be with some other brighter kids. Kids who had the same feelings as me… Well maybe not all the same feelings as me because I always like to be right so that wouldn't work out would it? I would like more friends who are children (but they'd have to let me be the dominant lion in our pride). Here, the teachers are more like my friends (which is weird because I thought teachers were meant to be pupils' arch enemies!)'

He also accepted that there were times when his reactions or behaviour complicated situations. He said, 'I can understand how hard it must be to put up with me sometimes if I look back on some of the things I've done, but humans were never put on this earth to succeed at everything. You just have to try your best.'

He did develop an awareness of PDA as a distinct condition, separate but fitting within the 'autism spectrum'. This allowed him to understand more about why he was at a school with other children who appeared quite different to him, but who were affected by issues in similar areas in their own unique way. When he was explaining his understanding of PDA to a member of staff, he said, 'What's PDA? Well the clue is in the name. It means if someone asks me to do something, I'm likely to say no…that's me all over isn't it?! But I'm also like a cat. It all depends on how you ask me. If you ask me in the right way, it's like stroking a cat's fur the way it grows. I may even purr! But if you ask me the wrong way, it's like stroking a cat's fur backwards. I'm likely to hiss!'

Some children with PDA are placed in schools for children with social, behavioural and emotional difficulties. On some occasions, this is because the needs of the child with PDA have been wrongly understood in the first place. On other occasions, it may be because aspects of that school's provision are felt to be most suitable for this particular child's needs. Notwithstanding what has been said about the personality and ethos of a school being more important than its designation, our own experience is that children with PDA, in most cases, tend to do very badly in this sort of placement. This is because the underlying reasons behind their behaviour are frequently misunderstood and misinterpreted. As well as this, the child with PDA will often copy or mimic some of the less desirable behaviour of other children and can be easily led or set up.

STATUTORY ASSESSMENT AND STATEMENTS OF SPECIAL EDUCATIONAL NEEDS

Whether or not a formal assessment, which may lead to a Statement of Special Educational Needs, is required is a concern to many parents when they are considering a school for their child. Just as there is variation in the way different local authorities organise their provision, the same is true in some of the ways that they assess and determine children's needs. This is particularly the case in their attitudes towards statutory assessments and the proportion of children within different authorities who receive a Statement of Special Educational Needs. Most children with SEN will have their needs met in their local schools and within that school's budget. Local authorities will then have different mechanisms for providing additional support or resources directly to the school if they are judged to be necessary. In what the SEN Code of Practice describes as 'a very small number of cases' the local authority will need to carry out a statutory assessment of special educational needs and then consider whether or not to issue a Statement of Special Educational Needs.

The whole area of statutory assessments and statements is complex, with clear legal duties placed on local authorities, prescribed timescales for completing certain processes, and mechanisms for appeal should there be disagreement. The assessment process aims to specify the individual needs of the child and the type of provision that is required to meet those needs. The Statement itself may specify the types and level of any additional support required, the arrangements for monitoring progress and the type and name of school where the provision is to be made. It is not within the scope of this book to describe these processes in any detail. The DCSF has published a summary booklet called *Special Educational Needs: A Guide for Parents and Carers* (DCSF 2009b) and comprehensive information is contained within the SEN Code of Practice itself which is available through the Department for Education website (www.education.gov.uk). Many local authorities also publish their own information and guidance and the local Parent Partnership Services (PPS) can be a good source of advice. The National Autistic Society (NAS) also offers detailed information on its website (www.autism.org.uk).

Many parents find the whole process legalistic and stressful, adding to the strain of caring for their child. While there is an emphasis in the Code of Practice on working in partnership with parents, a considerable number of families feel that it increases conflict and can undermine the good working relationships they have established with individual professionals.

Some individual parents such as Sandy Row (2005) and Ellen Power (2010) have written their own accounts of what they see as 'surviving the special educational needs system'; one describing herself as a 'velvet bulldozer' and the other a 'guerrilla mum'. Parents will benefit from support and advice if they are going through the process and again their local PPS may be helpful as a starting point. The NAS website includes an education rights section, which contains advice on issues such as preparing for meetings and writing letters. It also offers telephone support lines providing education advice and support with SEN Tribunals.

Unsurprisingly, there is considerable variation in the quality of Statements produced at the end of the process. In the best cases they are well written, accurately describe the child's needs, clearly specify the provision that is required and how this will be monitored, and reflect a consensus of all those involved in drawing it up. Sadly, this is not always the case, and they can be poorly written, inconsistent, contain out-of-date advice and be vague in the way they describe the provision that is required to meet a child's needs. In spite of the complexity of the process, and the stress that it may cause, many parents feel that this is outweighed by the advantages that a well-written and constructed Statement can bring in terms of setting out and protecting their child's entitlement to the provision specified.

This section has given an outline of the process that was in place at the time of writing. At the time of going to press the SEND green paper was undergoing consultation and a number of details are likely to change. The organisations listed in Appendix 1 for parents to contact to get further information will be able to offer advice in light of these changes.

EXCLUSIONS

A significant number of children with PDA have an educational history that is punctuated by multiple and sometimes lengthy periods of exclusion. This may be in the form of internal exclusion from the classroom, from partaking in various school activities or only being able to attend school for part of the day. It may also be as part of a formal exclusion on a temporary or permanent basis. This is a shameful situation that affects children across the autism spectrum and is often illegal. In 2007 a report was published by the Constructive Campaigning Parent Support Project entitled *Disobedience or Disability? The Exclusion of Children with Autism from Education*. The publication was based on a survey of parents from ten different local authorities and noted that 43 per cent of parents reported that their child had been officially excluded within the previous 12 months and that 53 per cent of parents noted instances of unofficial exclusion. Cases of unofficial, or informal, exclusions were often when parents were asked to remove their child before the end of the day and typically involved phone calls when they were asked to pick up their child from school as they were said to be finding a particular lesson or activity difficult. Parents most often felt that this reflected the fact that the school did not feel able to deal with the child's specific needs and occurred as a reactive response to critical incidents.

The report goes on to describe how these exclusions were often linked to particular times, for example the run-up to Christmas or events such as school trips or inspections. This mirrors our experience with many families of children with PDA and runs completely counter to any definition of inclusion. This is not to say that for some children, on some occasions, decisions might be taken between parents and school staff that a particular event or activity may be too stressful for the child and alternative arrangements need to be made. Nor that part-time attendance might not be in the child's best interest, perhaps as part of a gradual transition into school. Too often, though, incidences of exclusion occur without any detailed analysis and discussion of whether a child would manage the experience and what would be needed to enable them to do so. The fact that pupils might need particular support should not be a reason for their exclusion, which denies them opportunities for learning and new experiences.

In most situations the exercise of exclusion for children with PDA seems particularly futile. The behaviour that the school is finding challenging is most likely to be driven by the child's anxiety about aspects of the learning environment. If the child is then collected from school, or excluded for a period as a result, there is a real danger that this will only reinforce their behaviour and they will learn that it becomes an effective way of avoiding expectations. Often, parents in this situation can be too accepting of these episodes of exclusion or part-time attendance. Sometimes they are worried about 'rocking the boat' and feel that they risk permanent exclusion if they dispute the school's course of action by pointing out their child's entitlement to a full-time education. Ideally these situations can be resolved by discussions at the school and local authority level, but if parents feel they need access to independent advice a good source of information and advice is the Advisory Centre for Education (www.ace-ed.org.uk).

PERSONALISED PACKAGES OF SUPPORT

For some children with PDA, their educational history comprises a series of exclusions and placement breakdowns that can span both mainstream and specialist provision. For a few, it may be the case that all concerned agree that a particular child finds school so stressful, and his behaviour is so demanding, that he is best suited to a personalised package of learning and support. Local services may have different arrangements for delivering such programmes, either through their own service or commissioned from a voluntary provider. Provision may comprise elements of education and social care as part of the package. The programme might include working with the child at home, in the community and for part of the week within a school setting for particular aspects of the curriculum. For some children, this sort of package may also be a stepping-stone towards a transition back to school. Core elements of a successful package would include a high level of support, experience within the team of children with ASD/PDA, good leadership and co-ordination of different elements of the package, and a diverse and individualised curriculum.

Alice was already in her third mainstream school placement by Year 4 (aged 9). At this time, she was largely being taught in a separate room to the other children. She was often not in school at all, either due to difficulties regarding behaviour and co-operation when getting her there from home, or due to her parents being asked to collect her early because of disruptive and destructive behaviour. Both professionals and parents felt by the start of Year 5 (ages 9–10) that her needs would be better met at a specialist school for children on the autism spectrum. Even though this represented a potential compromise of her academic and social opportunities, it was the preferred choice for the sake of her emotional well-being.

She made good progress at the specialist school in terms of rebuilding her self-esteem as well as renewing her motivation to be in school where she was learning once again. For three years this placement worked well in many respects. The highly individualised timetable helped her to make academic progress, and the positive relationships she had with school staff helped to improve her self-confidence and personal development. Her explosive behaviour persisted. Although it had decreased in school, this was less the case at home. This presented challenges to her family as well as risk to her three younger siblings. She expressed a desire to stretch her science curriculum, and frustration with the lack of laboratory resources at the specialist school. Alice and her family hoped that she could find friendships with more able youngsters than the pupils at the specialist school. These were among the reasons that her parents, supported by the local authority, took the very difficult decision to move Alice to a residential school.

Alice moved to the residential special school in Year 8, aged 12, following a well-supported transition. Initially there was a positive settling-in period. Alice continued to have a personalised timetable and a variety of extra-curricular interests, and built relationships with some other pupils. She was able to make many of her own choices regarding what she did, how and when. The balance between staff boundaries and making decisions herself was difficult to sustain, however. After two terms it became clear that this setting was not meeting her needs nor was it sustainable as a placement. She was staying up much of the night, not attending many lessons, regularly planning and often carrying out destructive excursions around the school site in collaboration with other pupils, and sometimes absconding to steal goods from local shops.

Six months after having started at the residential school, Alice was excluded and moved back home without an alternative school placement. Her mother gave up her job at this point and worked together with the local authority to put some purposeful and positive structure in place for Alice. She had four morning sessions a week, at home, during which she continued to access some numeracy and literacy based on personal interests, some time to develop her hobbies, particularly playing the guitar, and opportunities to access the local community. During this break from school, Alice's family were able to establish a degree of stability to family routines and expectations. There continued to be flashpoints of behaviour that posed a risk to the well-being of those within the home, and a variety of accommodations needed to be made to family life.

Over the following few months a personalised package of education was put in place for Alice funded by the local authority, working in partnership with her parents. She began to attend a nearby centre for additional tutoring. Most of the tutorial centre's other pupils attended after school hours, which meant that the centre was very quiet during the day. Initially, Alice attended four morning sessions at the centre with her familiar teachers who had been working with her at home. They gradually handed over their teaching role to the centre's own staff. On the fifth day of the week she continued to have guitar lessons plus opportunities to increase her independence, problem solving and responsibility by spending time out in the community. In addition, she had weekly sessions with a nominated 'tutor' to work through issues related to her emotional well-being and personal development. Staff from a specialist school nearby offered regular guidance and consultation to the staff at the tutorial centre on an outreach basis. The time she spent at the tutorial centre was slowly increased, as was the range of activities she accessed there. A year later, she was able to attend the centre full time. She continued to play the guitar, she planned and enjoyed a number of experiences in the community, she had built positive relationships with staff and was able to moderate her explosive behaviour more often when at home. Her mother was able to go back to work, and Alice's relationships with her siblings improved. She had a good friendship with another child at the centre. She was making good progress academically in chemistry, music and maths and hoped to complete formal exams in these subjects. She had begun to increase her practical skills regarding cookery and gardening.

Alice's mother says that she can't regret the decisions they made for Alice earlier in her school career because they gave careful thought to making what they believed to be the best choices at the time. However, she now thinks that traditional schooling was probably never going to be the right path for Alice and is greatly comforted to have found a package that suits Alice and makes it possible for her to continue to live with her family.

HOME TEACHING

Home education is an alternative provision for any child and may sometimes be a useful one for the child or young person with PDA, at least for a period of time. While it may be an option, it is not an easy one and many parents of children and young people with PDA feel that their child's attendance at school may be the only respite they achieve. It may feel like a last resort after a string of failed placements, creating financial hardship and feelings of resentment towards an education system that has failed them and their child. This 'last resort' option is not ideal, as it may not be beneficial for either parent, child or their relationship. For some parents, though, it is a positive choice to home educate, and it may, in fact, be the best option for them.

It is the flexibility of educating at home which may suit a child or young person with PDA, who may not be able to follow the rigid approach and curriculum which is in place in many mainstream environments. It is sometimes a necessity for some parents whose children may be too anxious even to leave the house or are recurrent school refusers. There are few legal obligations to fulfil regarding educating at home, although the details of these are extremely variable throughout the country. Generally, as long as parents are open and co-operative with the educational authorities, the syllabus parents choose is up to them. Concerns about social and emotional development are cited in arguments against home education, and this can be a real issue. Often, though, there are local home education groups who meet regularly and might fulfil these aspects of a child's development. It may also be possible to provide social opportunities for a child in out-of-school activities if these are easier for him to tolerate.

CONCLUDING REMARKS

This chapter has emphasised that choosing, and providing, the best educational setting is less about the designation of an individual school than it is about the commitment and willingness to be adaptable and flexible in meeting the needs of the individual child. It is also important to bear in mind that different provision may well be appropriate at a different stage in a child's educational history. For example, if a child moves from a mainstream to a special school this might not be because the mainstream provision has 'failed' the child but because he needs something different at this stage of his education.

Finding the most appropriate school and making the appropriate provision can be very difficult for many children with PDA. However, effective provision can be made across the whole range of placements and the chapter has given examples from different settings as well as the key issues that are central to achieving this.

APPENDIX: QUESTIONS FOR PARENTS TO ASK WHEN VISITING SCHOOLS

Quite a lot of information can be obtained in advance through looking at the school's prospectus and inspection reports, which are likely to be available through the school's website. All schools are required to have written information on a range of topics, and you are likely to be particularly interested in their SEN policy, behaviour policy and those dealing with equal opportunities, bullying and exclusions.

You will be able to tell a lot from the initial welcome you get when you first approach a school to obtain information or arrange a visit. You will quite quickly get a feel for the school's ethos or character. Pay attention for evidence of positive attitudes towards all children and the sense in which they are valued as individuals. You will also get a feel for the way parents are included by the manner in which your questions are responded to.

Many parents find it helpful to visit with a friend, or perhaps a professional whose view they value, and who also knows their child. At some stage you are likely to want your child to visit, but usually on the first visit you are likely to find that you can feel more relaxed and concentrate on the questions you want to ask without the child being there.

You may want to consider, or ask, specific questions about some of the following:

- Has the school had previous experience of teaching children with ASD/PDA?

- What training have the staff received recently about the condition and are they prepared to update this if necessary?

- If my child were to start at the school, which class would they be in? What is the peer group in that class? What staffing levels are available and would my child receive any additional support?

- How are children supported at lunch times and play times?

- Does the school have access to specialist advice from an outreach team or visiting therapists?

- How will the school make sure that all staff understand my child's needs?

- What happens if my child doesn't co-operate or becomes angry or disruptive?

- What systems are in place for drawing up my child's Individual Education Plan? How will the curriculum be differentiated if needed?

- How will the school ensure my child has access to all areas of the curriculum and school life, including out-of-school visits, for example?

- What are the school's usual arrangements for parents to come in and discuss their child? What systems are in place to support home/school communication, including the provision of written reports?

- How will the other children be supported to understand my child's needs? Are there any specific strategies adopted by the school to support positive peer relationships?

Chapter 5

DEVELOPING EMOTIONAL WELL-BEING AND SELF-AWARENESS IN CHILDREN WITH PDA

Recognising the underlying source of any behaviour plays an important part in helping to decide how to deal with it. Adults tend to choose strategies which match their interpretation of events. For instance, a child refusing to co-operate with a request could be explained as wilful and inconsiderate, or as anxious and confused. The adult assuming the first analysis, is likely to become more forceful and demanding and to start to use threats of punishments. The adult assuming the second, is more likely to reassure, explain and negotiate. The assumption which will probably be most appropriate for children with PDA, is that the child may be anxious and confused.

Whereas children with PDA may recognise emotions, and in this respect can be markedly different from children with autism, there is a feeling that this is superficial, and they have difficulty sharing emotions or connecting with feelings. This is discussed in Chapter 1. Although children with PDA may have difficulty connecting with their own and other people's emotional states, they can nonetheless be deeply affected by them. They may have difficulty taking responsibility for their own actions, struggle to develop a deeper sense of empathy and to control their impulses, yet at the same time, have a strong sense of justice. They may respond inappropriately or explosively and may find it hard to learn from previous experiences. For those people living and working with children with PDA, the characteristics of the child which usually stand out are a focus on avoiding co-operation and being controlling and an empathy which lacks depth. For the children themselves, however, central features of their differences are often characterised by anxiety and low self-esteem. Over time, this can erode their emotional well-being and have a negative impact on their self-image.

Chapter 2 outlines a number of strategies designed to reduce a child's anxiety by adapting and managing their immediate environment. This chapter focuses on the impact of anxiety in terms of children's longer-term emotional well-being and developing self-awareness. It will also outline some ways to further develop personal understanding.

In recent years, throughout the UK, there has been increasing emphasis in educational policy and practice on recognising mental health needs and promoting emotional well-being in all children. This has included: Healthy Schools initiatives (since 1999), Every Child Matters (DfES 2004), Social and Emotional Aspects of Learning (DCSF 2007) and the New Ofsted Framework (Ofsted 2009).

In 2010, the National Autistic Society (NAS) published a document called *You Need to Know* investigating the impact of mental health problems on children with ASD and their families. The report focused on what can be done to improve the outcomes and experiences of these families, including making some recommendations to other agencies as well as government, to promote the well-being of this group. It was reported that '9 out of 10 parents [said] that mental health problems faced by their child had had a negative impact on their own mental health (88%) and on the family as a whole (91%)'. The report also referred to the findings of Simonoff E. *et al.* (2008) that 71 per cent of children with autism develop mental health problems compared to a prevalence rate of around 10 per cent in other children.

This recent recognition of the increased fragility of emotional well-being for children on the autism spectrum has a beneficial impact for supporting children with PDA, not only within school systems but also for other agencies which may be involved with a family.

In Chapter 1, the key characteristics of the child as a learner were outlined. Based on some of these characteristics, children with PDA may experience particularly fragile emotional well-being because of the *impact* of some of these characteristics, as is set out in Table 5.1.

Table 5.1 Emotional impact of some key characteristics of children with PDA

Characteristic	Impact on emotional well-being
A need to be in control	→ Anxiety about real, perceived or anticipated demands being made
Explosive behaviour	→ Damage to relationships with peers as well as to self-esteem
Difficulty co-operating and practising skills	→ Poor sense of achievement and low self-esteem
Desire to be on par or better than others but not seeing the effort necessary to develop skills	→ Low self-esteem and difficulty occupying free time constructively as it can be hard to develop skills and hobbies
Desire to have friendships and relationships with other children but either inadvertently sabotaging this or being socially vulnerable	→ Feeling isolated socially and lacking deep, lasting reciprocal relationships
Ambivalence about succeeding or enjoying an experience or activity	→ Development of negative associations with succeeding or co-operating, and sometimes being a harsh judge of their own achievements
Unrealistically high standards of themselves and also sometimes of other people	→ Feeling let down by others and being prone to low self-esteem regarding own achievements
Lack of permanence and transfer of skills	→ Occasional dramatic setbacks which damage self-esteem, require re-learning and re-establishing relationships of trust
Poor emotional regulation and variability in behaviour	→ Mood swings which bring stress to the child and those around him; difficulties relaxing or coping with excitement or anxiety
Difficulty interpreting own emotions	→ Emotional confusion and frustration
Difficulty compromising, accommodating others and empathising	→ Feeling frustrated and misunderstood, which can lead to conflict
Difficulty predicting, reflecting and understanding cause and effect	→ Feeling taken by surprise by some events or outcomes; tendency to make unwise risk assessments or judgement calls
Difficulty taking responsibility for own actions	→ Frustration regarding perceived injustices, or even feeling victimised

HOW CAN EMOTIONAL WELL-BEING FOR CHILDREN WITH PDA BE APPROACHED WITHIN SCHOOLS?

In the light of the recent government initiatives in the UK, there is increased scope for schools to include this work within their provision. As described in Chapter 1, one school which has done this is Sutherland House School. The school has taken a holistic approach to education, putting an emphasis on approaches which prioritise communication and interaction (Christie *et al.* 1992; Christie and Wimpory 1986). Historically, these approaches have included Musical Interaction and Intensive Interaction as well as relaxation, yoga, occupational therapy and speech and language therapy. Following discussion between senior staff at the school, the governing body and parents, a system of *personal tutorials* was developed across the school to address emotional well-being for all pupils. The key objective was to secure protected time for individual sessions that could encompass interactive work, the development of self-awareness and for some pupils, where appropriate, discussions about their own condition and diagnosis. The key principles behind the approach are that tutorials:

- are open to all pupils

- prioritise interaction

- keep the child at the centre of approaches and pace

- consult and involve parents

- provide training and support for staff involved in the process.

A more detailed description of this approach working with children and young people across the autism spectrum was published in *Good Autism Practice* (Christie *et al.* 2008).

WHAT IS A PERSONAL TUTORIAL?

Personal tutorials are typically 1:1 sessions between a pupil and their nominated tutor, preferably on a weekly basis, but sometimes fortnightly. They usually happen somewhere quiet and away from the busy classroom environment, are ideally uninterrupted and will last for anything from 30 to 60 minutes.

Tutors are, in the main, members of staff who have key roles within the pupil's class group, but occasionally these are staff who have been deliberately chosen because their current role is slightly removed from the pupil's everyday school situation (e.g. this may be a more senior staff member, a therapist or a member of the pupil's previous class who continues as their tutor while they settle into a new class). Matching pupils to tutors is done carefully and should take into consideration individual pupil needs and personality, staff expertise, pupil choice (where appropriate), as well as timetable availability. Personal tutorials do not necessarily have to happen with therapists or professionals with particular qualifications. They rely heavily on relationships with an adult who has a good intuitive grasp of the child's needs and personality, whatever their role within school. Positive relationships are critical in working effectively with children with PDA so this match between child and tutor needs to be carefully monitored and supported. Chapter 2 highlights the importance of building relationships between staff and children with PDA, including discussing positive style and approaches.

It is a crucial feature of effective tutorials that the underlying principles of the approach are understood. To this end, it is recommended that all staff delivering tutorials have attended training as well as receive ongoing supervision. It is helpful to have a designated team of experienced staff working across the school who can give advice and support. These members of staff can also observe sessions and monitor the effectiveness of tutorials.

It is essential for tutors to understand their role. This is to provide a supportive, non-judgemental, interactive environment, which facilitates social and emotional development. Achieving this means that tutors often need to focus on their style. A key skill for tutors to develop is a sensitive use of pace and timing within the session. This requires them carefully to gauge the child's motivation alongside any anxiety so that they time when to move on from a topic, when to make a request, when to explore a new activity, when to use humour and when to reassure. They can also use the pace of their interaction to allow for pauses. Children with PDA can need more processing time for a number of reasons; giving more time can allow for any delayed processing of language, it can give the child time to co-operate with a demand (however small) being made, and using dramatic pauses can also contribute to sustaining a child's engagement by adding a sense of intrigue. One pupil who was used to having personal tutorials described the ideal tutor as someone who 'is trustworthy and encourages you. They should like you for who you are and have a sense of humour. They should encourage you and be interested in what you think but not put you under pressure.'

Working in this way with children with PDA can be as rewarding as it is challenging. It offers adults opportunities to use their creativity and base the content of the sessions on what motivates and interests the child.

HOW ARE TUTORIALS EXPLAINED TO CHILDREN?

Tutorials are explained to children as sessions which give them opportunities to play and to talk, to help them to relax, to understand friendships, to think about their choices or preferences and to help them plan for growing up. As a general guide, it can be helpful to use a range of everyday materials during conversations with children with PDA. These can serve the purposes of distracting and de-personalising, and in some cases they can add an alternative way of expressing their thoughts. For example, using a toy animal or doll can not only soften the pressure of a direct request, but can also be used to ask or answer questions. Sometimes a child may feel more open and relaxed when expressing their thoughts or feelings through a neutral 'third party' in this way. Using pens and paper can make it easier for the adult to let a game of noughts and crosses slip into doodling, which can, in turn, slip into drawing cartoon characters or diagrams. In this situation, it is important that the movement between the different stages of such a conversation is as smooth as possible. These diagrams or cartoons can include comic strip use of thought or speech bubbles, or can develop into graded scales of different emotions. Carol Gray's *Comic Strip Conversations* (1994) uses illustration to teach social understanding. Kari Dunn Buron and Mitzi Curtis's *Incredible 5-Point Scale* (2003) uses scales to develop understanding of social interaction and to help control emotional responses to difficult situations. Similarly, some ordinary family games can clearly illustrate the effects of overload or anxiety. Good examples of these games are Jenga (where a wooden tower is made increasingly unstable by taking turns to remove support blocks) or Buckaroo (where players take turns to hang items off the saddle of a horse until the weight of them makes him buck them all off).

Children are encouraged to contribute to planning the content of their tutorials, suggesting games or activities. For children with PDA this shared control is a key feature of promoting co-operation. The most crucial initial goal when starting tutorials must be to build rapport. A relationship where there is good rapport is one which is characterised by a positive social and emotional connection between two people. This is important for all children but more so for children with PDA, and should be prioritised over other goals in the initial stages. That is not to say that they are sessions without any boundaries or guidance, but that the focus of the adult's style is to facilitate rather than to direct. This is what sets tutorials aside from most other 'teaching' sessions.

WHAT HAPPENS DURING A PERSONAL TUTORIAL?

It is key to the effectiveness of personal tutorials that the child should feel at ease and motivated to participate in the sessions. Developing this can take time and intuitive skill. The child should be able to lead while the adult guides and facilitates. The adult should be constantly reassessing and 'adjusting the dials' (see Figure 2.1) of the balance between the child's tolerance and the adult's demand. While the tone of personal tutorials is being established, it can be helpful to use personal interests and relaxation techniques. There may be many significant themes which need exploring during personal tutorials, but judging the pace and timing of them is critical. It may take many weeks of sessions to establish sufficient trust and rapport before sensitive issues can be raised. The benefits of doing so in the early stages should not be underestimated as it contributes greatly to future effectiveness.

Some of the examples below illustrate how a variety of issues have been worked through in personal tutorials. It must be noted, however, that there will have been many weeks and months of building rapport with these pupils before getting to the point of exploring certain topics. In the early weeks, during which the sessions provide time to play favourite games or use books or magazines reflecting particular interests, small-scale personal projects may feature which are useful to motivate and engage children without them feeling under pressure. For example, a conversation which happens while cooking, or making a papier-mâché model can feel less intense to the child and work towards establishing a positive relationship. The following examples will have had to be introduced carefully within the context of judging the right moment even on that particular day. Also, they may be significant moments but may represent only a small part of the whole tutorial.

Establishing trust and confidentiality

Establishing trust has already been described as fundamental to successful interaction with children with PDA. Within personal tutorials, this respect can be reinforced by using a system which demonstrates trustworthiness. During one of Dylan's (aged 12) tutorials, there was a conversation about deciding which information or thoughts are private or personal and which are OK to share. Together, some different categories were developed which let him keep control of how he organised information. The only reason his categories could be overridden was if not to do so would put him or someone else at risk of harm. This meant that after something had been discussed, he could decide how to sort the information. The categories were:

- *Public information*
  This is information which can be shared with anyone who knows you. It includes straightforward facts, such as you are a boy or you have brown eyes, as well as other information which you are happy for anyone to know, such as you support Nottingham Forest football club or you hate broccoli.

- *Personal information*
  This is information that a few people may know and may need to talk to you and to each other about in order to help you. It will include information that they will need to be careful not to share

with people who may use this information to upset or harm you. It may be information such as, you are worried about growing up, you are scared of Doctor Who monsters and sometimes you have nightmares about them, you are not ready to tell other boys at scouts that you have additional needs. We can decide together who should and shouldn't know any particularly sensitive information.

- *Private information*
  This is information that only you know at the moment. It includes the thoughts you have in your head that you have not told anyone. Everyone has some private thoughts, and there can be different reasons why they have not told other people their thoughts. Some thoughts are neutral ideas, such as what your favourite colour is. Others may be more confidential, such as what you think about when you are on your own or how you feel about needing to sleep with cuddly toys at night. It might be a good idea if you did talk to someone about these ideas. If other people do know some of this private information, it is important that they understand the need to be sensitive when they talk to you about them and who else they tell. (This can then lead on to discussions about how to know who are the best people to talk to about sensitive subjects.)

It was in the context of such conversations that the drawing opposite was made.

It is also important to recognise how this relationship of trust and rapport between personal tutor and child can have benefits beyond the actual tutorial sessions. There are times when, even though adults have made every effort to avoid a confrontation, a meltdown becomes inevitable. It needs to be accepted by adults that it is not possible to defuse every flashpoint.

When a meltdown does happen, what matters is how adults then handle it. It is of course helpful to use a lot of the strategies already outlined in earlier chapters (e.g. reducing demands, de-personalising, etc.). But it is really useful to remember that one of the most powerful strategies already available is the relationships that key adults have with a child. Once any issues regarding immediate safety have been dealt with, a child may be

He pushed me.

"When you have a secret, it builds
like a ring of fire around you which
gets hotter and hotter, and closer and
closer. In the end you have to
put the fire out by telling
someone. You have to tell the right
person or it can get worse."

ready to talk. This is when the 'scaffolding' of work done in personal tutorials can be supportive. Adults who have positive relationships with children, and who make those children feel accepted and understood, are ideally placed to reassure and help the children move on from a difficult situation. In fact, seeing a child through a difficult incident in a supportive and non-judgemental way can even contribute to the bond that a child has with key adults.

Using drawings and other visual means to explore concepts

Children with PDA find it easier to respond to requests which are not directive or confusing. Using visual strategies to explore concepts requiring social and emotional understanding can be useful for de-personalising a demand while adding clarity to abstract ideas.

Duncan (aged 11) has been described in Chapter 2. He is an articulate, engaging youngster who struggles with mood swings. Sometimes these mood swings take even him by surprise and can be as difficult for him to control as they are for adults to manage safely. He is uncomfortable with, and at times suspicious of, conversations which try to probe his emotions. During a tutorial, however, he was able to draw how being cross felt to him.

Starting at the left-hand side, he said 'cross' built like a swirl, then erupted into a volcano which spilt its lava into a boiling river before it calmed. He was able to draw his feelings and describe the drawing in an articulate and meaningful way, but would have found communicating this idea using only verbal skills too difficult and therefore too demanding.

Dylan (aged 12) had episodes of being troubled by recurring bad dreams at night and upsetting thoughts during the day. He did not talk about these worries for many months, but within the context of a personal tutorial, he was able to draw the thoughts represented by what he called 'worry monsters' (see the illustrations of the three monsters opposite, which he named the 'crashing aeroplane monster', the 'scared of the dark monster' and the 'fear of stinging nettles monster'). It was also important to liaise with his family as these worries were causing particular difficulty regarding him falling asleep at night. He did not believe that these monsters *were* the worries, but was using them as metaphors. This revealed how well he was doing with his conceptual understanding and it also gave a visual way to explore and provide strategies to help.

At the start of this work, the monsters he drew were colourful, menacing, strong and large (see p.151). Following a couple of months of work using role play, drawing comic strips with outcomes Dylan could control, writing scripts for what he could tell the monsters when they came bothering him, developing distraction techniques and trying to disempower the monsters by talking about them, Dylan re-drew monsters over time to show how they had diminished in size and influence, such as in the drawing below.

Dylan is a very creative child who has a keen interest in story writing and drawing. If the balance between the degree of demand and his motivation is paced well by the supporting adult, he can be comfortable co-operating with using pens and paper, because of this interest. However, if he picks up a tone of 'therapy' or 'interview', this co-operation can soon evaporate.

He did the drawing opposite to illustrate the point he wanted to make about opportunities. The person at the bottom of the picture is the character representing 'Life Opportunities'. Dylan is the person at the top of the picture. He explained his drawing like this: 'Life has lots of arms because he can throw lots of opportunities at you, but you can only catch and hold one or two at any one time. The problem is, how do I know which opportunities to catch and which to drop if something more important comes along?'

He was making a very valid observation reflecting his developing maturity and self-awareness which gave a model to refer back to when he needed help making decisions such as what to choose to spend his pocket money on, or which film to see. As decision making becomes more complex, this idea can still apply.

Using images, analogies and metaphors to illustrate a point can be helpful to children with PDA. This is because they provide a way to explore concepts using familiar ideas but without being directly related to the child himself. Children with PDA may be able to 'see the point' within a story but sometimes struggle to make the connection between the principle and how it applies to themselves. This does mean it is not a helpful approach, and assumptions should not be made that the child has understood that the teaching point is directly relevant to them.

Duncan used drawings of jigsaw pieces to illustrate his perception of friendships and relationships. His drawing showed that he had an awareness of needing a certain degree of making a 'good match' within a relationship. By using his own analogy, it was then possible to explore further conversations about 'good enough' matches rather than 'perfect matches', and to introduce some ideas of accommodating other people's needs and priorities.

Edwin (aged 9) has an appealing character along with a great capacity for concentration and problem solving regarding topics which interest him (such as wind turbines). He has a strong sense of justice and wants to have friends. There are often difficulties between him and his classmates when he feels that he has not been prioritised or treated fairly.

He drew the picture opposite to illustrate how hard he feels that he is trying to make friends and how he views the other people who say they are his friends. In the picture, he is trying to build a wind turbine. He has already made the considerable effort of climbing the ladder up the tower and is standing on the top ready to direct other people. One blade is in place belonging to his younger sister (i.e. she has been supportive and helpful). Another blade is being lifted by the crane. Edwin's friends (Sam and Dylan) are on the ground thinking of stopping the building work or going to do something different (i.e. not doing what Edwin had in mind). He views this as sabotage, unfairness and disloyalty. The fairy godmother in the top right corner is the school class teacher (who may well sometimes wish for a magic wand, trying to keep the peace between them all).

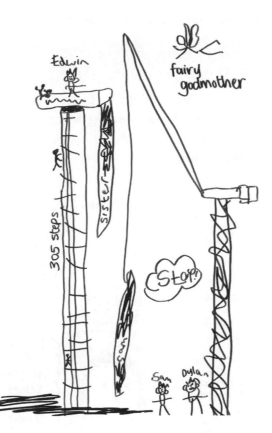

Developing problem-solving strategies

Before anyone can apply problem-solving strategies effectively, a problem itself needs to be identified. The better the understanding of the nature of that problem, the more appropriate the choice of strategy to deal with it. For instance, you may be feeling short-tempered, frustrated and inclined to snap at your work colleagues. You feel that you are overworked and undervalued and maybe it's time you told other people so. You wonder whether to ask to talk to your boss right here and now. However, you may actually be feeling like this today because you are over-tired, have a headache and you have a work deadline approaching. You are free to choose option 1: to have it out with your boss and resign from your job. Alternatively, you could also decide on option 2: to take a painkiller, have an early night and put off any major decision making until the next day. Even if you revert to option 1 the following day, you may approach it in a more balanced way.

A personal tutorial was used to explore similar themes of overload for Neesha (aged 10) who had become increasingly agitated as the day wore on and had then got 'stuck'. She had withdrawn all co-operation from lessons or complying with simple requests and was also refusing to go home at the end of the day (despite school being the place she least wanted to be by that time). She had become overtaken by a series of simultaneous events and emotions and was struggling even to identify them, let alone resolve them. Her personal tutor did this drawing to illustrate what was on her mind.

She was worried because her friend Peter was unwell that day and was not his usual self. Neesha had decided she wanted to follow a gluten-free diet (although this was not medically necessary) and there was no spare gluten-free bread at school. She had struggled to get herself ready for school in time that day (maybe, in hindsight, this was an indication it was a less tolerant day in general). She was frustrated that it was 'indoor playtime' because the grassy garden was too slippery and muddy from recent rain even though it was not *actually* raining at playtime. She felt that it was unfair that staff had the final word about choosing where to go on the school trip, not her. Finally, numeracy was her least favourite subject and that afternoon's lesson had been the 'straw that broke the camel's back'.

Once the various issues were demonstrated in a visual way, she was then able to sort them. For example, some problems had easy answers (such as buying more bread), some were not anyone's fault but still needed an appealing alternative solution (such as the rainy playtime), some were about managing her frustration by talking about it and by using relaxation techniques (this related to her feeling annoyed about being late, or dealing with numeracy). All of this process was supported by her personal tutor who knew her well, who had a good trusting relationship with her and who was skilled at presenting conversations in a non-judgemental, respectful and reassuring way.

There are many elements to this kind of problem solving. These include:

- recognising the type of problem it is

- deciding what degree of difficulty this problem presents

- developing a repertoire of strategies

- choosing the appropriate strategy for this situation.

In addition, there will be many smaller steps along the way. Solving practical problems is hard enough, but learning to solve social and emotional problems is very complex and a life-long process for everyone. Children with PDA are going to need additional support in developing these skills.

Grading emotions

Children with PDA often have difficulty regulating their emotions. They can tend to see things as all wonderful or all dreadful and struggle to appreciate 'shades of grey'. They can also swing from one extreme emotional state to another. This can take them by surprise as well as the people around them and can be very unsettling for everyone. Being able to grade emotions can encourage a better awareness of the degree of their feelings and can guide children towards using a strategy which is in keeping with that score. It can also help to prepare adults who live and work with children with PDA to plan their responses to given situations.

Catrina (aged 13), used the diagram below to give a score to each feeling on a day when all she could verbalise was that she was not feeling her usual self.

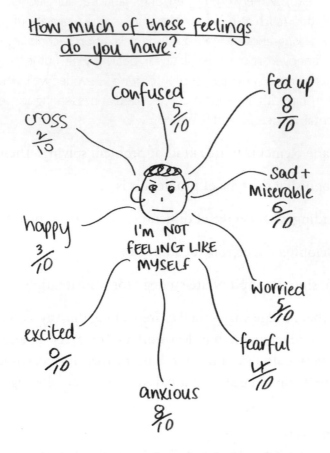

In working towards an awareness of grading feelings, Edwin created his own emotional barometer. There are many different adaptations and versions of this type of tool available, such as Kari Dunn Buron and Mitzi Curtis's (2003) work on the 'Incredible 5-Point Scale'.

Edwin decided on the labels for each category on his chart, and with his teacher, placed those labels into colour bands representing different degrees of intervention needed. This meant that sometimes, he would only need to say a colour or a number to indicate the level of difficulty he was experiencing. It was helpful for him to have a visual way of demonstrating not only how he felt at moments of explosive behaviour, but also to develop an awareness of when those moments were building, plus a sense of de-escalation when he was starting to calm down.

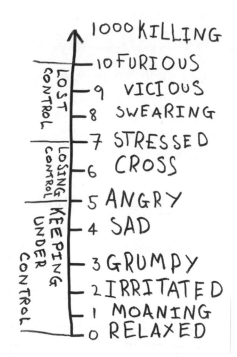

Over time, Edwin was encouraged to develop a variety of strategies to match these categories, ranging from distracting himself with a favourite comic to leaving the room to go to a safe designated area where he could stay, with an adult, until he feels calmer.

Making choices

Before children can make genuine choices, they need to understand the options which are available to them as well as having a sense of their attitude towards those options. This can present its own area of work for some children with PDA, where there can be a degree of pressure associated simply with making a choice, even if it is a choice about something they find rewarding. This means that gauging when to offer choice (to increase co-operation) and when to limit it (to decrease anxiety) can sometimes be a delicate and highly individualised balance.

Jenny (aged 15) had experienced a number of complicated school exclusions which had left her particularly socially isolated, nervous of new situations and very demand avoidant. She was anxious of being out in the community or of trying new activities, and would come up with a range of complex techniques to avoid finding herself in situations which may be uncomfortable to her. As she entered her late teens, she was spending most of her time in her bedroom, using computer games and making cardboard figures of the characters in her favourite games, often into the early hours of the morning. She had no other interests or hobbies yet she aspired to having qualifications and paid employment one day. Staff supporting her worked closely with Jenny's family to try to encourage her to regain her confidence in going out.

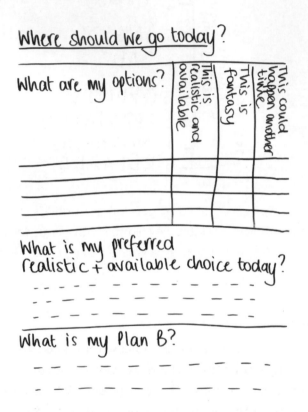

A personalised form was developed to use with Jenny to help her take some control and responsibility in planning outings. It was handwritten to make it appear less like formal school work; it allowed for some impossible fantasies in order to indulge a sense of humour as well as to reduce pressure; it allowed for a suggestion to be made which could be shelved until another time; and it built in a 'Plan B' in case of emergencies or unforeseen events. These unforeseen events may have been something like the cinema being closed for refurbishment, but equally they could have been that there were too many other school trips of young children at the museum so Jenny felt too crowded and needed to leave.

Making decisions can be hard for some children with PDA. Sometimes children can feel stuck because they can't cope with adults making decisions for them on the one hand, but equally can't cope with making a choice for themselves on the other. This can be extremely anxiety-provoking for some children. When 'stuck' in these moments, it can be often be wise to let the moment pass, recognising that to push the point is not going to be helpful to anyone. At these times, choices regarding immediate safety will obviously have to be seen through, but everyone can save face if a decision seems too hard to make and is postponed until a later date.

Understanding consequences

Another element of decision making is about taking responsibility for the consequences of choices that have been made. Some consequences are easier to predict than others, and some consequences are more rewarding than others. This whole process can be confusing and frustrating for children with PDA. Taking responsibility for actions presents a challenge to many children with PDA for a number of reasons. Doing so can be a reminder of whether they did, or did not, co-operate with a request, both of which can raise problems. Taking responsibility for your own actions requires an understanding of your own role in relation to other people. It may also carry an implication of higher expectations in the future; for example, if it is acknowledged that a different decision would have been better, there may be perceived pressure to comply or improve another time. Plus it requires an understanding of other people's emotions and intentions in order to apportion responsibility appropriately as well as to make sense of other people's reactions. This is often complicated for children with PDA. For these reasons, when trying to develop an understanding of responsibility for the consequences of one's actions, it is usually best to start with issues which have positive, rewarding outcomes. It can be helpful if this is within the context of praising a child in a way they find acceptable; for example, 'You are so strong, thank goodness you were there to help me unload the shopping from the car. Now that job has been done so quickly I have got some extra time to play with you.'

Dylan has a great interest in Doctor Who. In particular, he knows lots of information about the various alien enemies and their masters. This interest was used to illustrate a point about making strategic decisions and taking responsibility for them by picturing himself as a master. He will receive incoming suggestions from a number of his key advisers. They may give him good or bad advice and he may have better ideas of his own, but in the end, he has ultimate control of his own actions and choices. This gives a context to working towards taking responsibility for the consequences of those actions and choices.

When children have acted in a way that has negative consequences, there is a place for pointing this out as a teaching point, but it needs to be both well timed and done sensitively. Sometimes this is best done away from the heat of the moment, other times it can be useful to refer to it at the time, but then swiftly move on. Children with PDA are likely to know that something has gone wrong even if they are confused by some of the circumstances leading to it. It can be effective to talk about decisions they made which had negative outcomes as choices, for example:

You chose to throw your meal across the room. I understand that this dinner is not your favourite. When you don't like the dinner you have lots of choices. You can leave it on your plate, put it in the bin, ask for something else or throw it. They are all choices. Each one has a different result. Throwing your dinner makes… happen. Let's try another choice.

It can also be helpful to find a way of talking about having not made the best choices which allows them not to lose face, for example:

You have done so well to stay in this lesson even when you think that maths is boring. I know you're waiting to have your turn on the computer. Why don't you do half of these maths questions and I'll do the others then you can go to the computer? Now don't leave me all the hard ones, I'm not as good at maths as you are…

Teaching relaxation

Many children with PDA benefit from developing strategies to help them to relax. For some children it is too pressurising to teach them specific techniques which they are expected to use when they are stressed. In this instance, it may be up to the supporting adults to gently 'engineer' useful strategies at the right moment. They may range from distraction, maybe using personal interests or favourite pastimes, to exercise. For those children who may be encouraged to develop sufficient motivation, it can be helpful to teach yoga directly, but other children may need to learn some yoga techniques in order to 'teach yoga to someone else' as their way of doing it.

Getting involved in a hobby can be a good way of doing something absorbing and relaxing.

Declan became interested in playing the guitar (largely motivated initially by wanting to be rich and famous). He was not only able to stick with this as an interest but developed it into a very real skill. He was able to get so involved and absorbed in his playing that he could forget other things on his mind. He said: 'I like playing the guitar. It makes me feel happy… My eyes sometimes go blurred when I'm playing the guitar. I think it's because I'm concentrating. It's like I need glasses but I don't really… I'm proud of myself about how I've improved on the guitar.'

Being able to use playing an instrument in this way not only gave him something positive to do, but also contributed to better self-esteem. It also so happened to be something that over time he could do with or alongside other people which opened up social opportunities.

HOW TO ACHIEVE CO-OPERATION AND REFLECTION FROM CHILDREN WITH PDA

The examples of work above are useful illustrations of flexible and visual ways to help children with PDA express their thoughts, emotions and opinions. They do not have to be carried out by a trained specialist; parents or other adults with a good understanding of the child and who use the right approaches can work effectively in this way. Being effective will, of course, improve with experience and will be supported by suggestions in this book. It is as important to think back over things that are going well as to reflect on things which are raising difficulties. This is not just to celebrate achievements but also to improve awareness of which approaches work well for particular children.

It must be noted that by the time the moment was right to explore many of the examples in this chapter, these children had been having personal tutorial sessions for a number of weeks or even months. Developing social and emotional well-being is long-term work and needs to be allowed to evolve at the child's own pace. The adults in these examples had worked hard at developing relationships of trust with the children, and the pace and timing of each session was managed thoughtfully. Care was taken to monitor not only the mood of the moment, but the context of the day (e.g. Have they had a tough playtime today? Are they ill? Was it their worst school dinner today? Is the room too hot/cold?).

Opening up sensitive conversations with children with PDA can sometimes be helped by doing something slightly distracting, such as playing with Lego. If an adult uses an activity with a child while talking to them, it should be an activity which is sufficiently interesting to motivate the child while securing a level of co-operation. It is important, though, not to be so absorbing that it requires all their concentration, because this will reduce their capacity for exploring complicated conversations. Helpful activities can include construction sets, colouring, clay, making key rings/beads/jewellery, and cooking. Obviously, personal interests will guide suitable choices here.

Adults who are good at achieving co-operation are often adults who are aware of their own contribution to the mood of the moment. Adults who judge their pace and timing well and who are able to follow the child's lead are more successful at exploring sensitive topics. Adults who are calm and reassuring, who don't take things personally and who are able to wipe the slate clean as often as necessary are the adults who maintain engagement. These are the adults who are far more appealing to, as well as more effective in helping, children with PDA.

Having said that, these 'ideal adults' do not always get it right; and even when they do, will need support themselves. Children with PDA can be some of the most rewarding yet also some of the most challenging individuals to spend time with, and this is why all adults involved with them will need to work collaboratively and supportively. This has been discussed in more detail in Chapter 4.

PLANNING AND EVALUATING

Areas of focus

The nature of tutorial sessions relies heavily on shared control between the pupil and adult. In recognition of this, at Sutherland House where there is a system of personal tutorials in use across the school, there is not a target-driven way of assessing pupils' progress in this work. That is not to say that there is no planning done for tutorials, but that issues being addressed within the sessions are looked upon as 'areas of focus', rather than as specific aims or objectives. An 'area of focus' describes an overall aim and method without giving a prescribed target. The following could be some examples of areas of focus:

- to use cartoon drawing/doodling to explore themes of emotional understanding and empathy

- to use personalised, visual ways of recording what is important to him (e.g. mind maps, talking mats, lists)

- to extend his interest in film making to develop skills in using a video camera to make a video diary/interview others in order to encourage him to reflect back on previous experiences

- to devise a barometer of his moods using emotional vocabulary and trying to identify some potential triggers or flashpoints.

How is work in this area monitored and supported?

At one specialist school, the following model of monitoring supports the work done in personal tutorials. There are experienced members of staff with responsibility for supporting personal tutorials called 'designated supervisors' who work throughout the school. Each designated supervisor works to maintain the profile and standards of work done in personal tutorials and meets regularly with designated supervisors from other parts of the school. Together they monitor and develop good practice. The designated supervisors carry out their work under the guidance of an assistant head teacher who has overall responsibility for emotional well-being and whole-school development.

Staff working as personal tutors receive training regarding the ethos, style and content of tutorials, and discuss individual pupils at regular meetings. Personal tutorials are observed and monitored periodically not only to maintain standards but also to provide opportunities to develop work in terms of staff skills and pupil progress. Areas of focus are planned at the start of each term in consultation with other staff as appropriate. At the end of each term the areas of focus are evaluated, and at the end of each year they are reported on as part of each child's annual review.

Evaluation of personal tutorials

It is not straightforward for schools to measure progress and demonstrate outcomes in respect of emotional well-being. Some of the more significant evaluations are indicated by qualitative (subjective) comments rather than quantitative (measurable) data. Following consultation with pupils, parents and staff at Sutherland House School, the following comments reflect some responses to the work done and the priority given to emotional well-being.

PUPIL RESPONSE

Pupils commented on the importance and effectiveness of their personal tutorials:

I think of our (tutorial) time together as useful and interesting. Things are better for me now. I used to think I was the one who should change – I don't think that now. Now I think it's OK just to be me.

Tutorials are cool. They make you feel important. Everyone should have one.

Even if you are at your most depressed emotion, tutorials always help you feel better. Solving problems in your life is easier when you talk about it. It helps to rebuild your confidence after a difficult time.

PARENT RESPONSE

Parents commented on the strength and value of personal tutorials at school:

Personal tutorials give my child a regular opportunity to offload. It can be harder at home to talk about difficult issues without it becoming heated and personal. It is much better to share these conversations between more objective professionals at school, and his loving family at home.

The work done in personal tutorials is an essential part of my son's development. Without emotional well-being it's much more difficult to achieve any other progress.

Personal tutorials have provided a safe way of tackling some delicate issues which, if handled wrongly, would have been much more explosive!

Some parents have implemented this approach at home:

Regular personal tutorials at school have given a label to the kind of talking time that we try to have at bedtime at home. It has made it easier for him to accept a home 'Mum-torial' as opposed to a school tutorial.

STAFF RESPONSE
Staff show a clear commitment to the ethos and importance of this aspect of their work:

Having personal tutorials has been a vital tool to forming a good relationship with her. Without the trust and positive interaction that we developed during our sessions it would have been much more difficult, and certainly would have taken much longer, to get to a place where we can actually make progress.

It is very precious to have some nominated time where we can enjoy being together.

What I have learnt about what makes him tick in personal tutorials has made me better at teaching him in the classroom.

The relationship I have with her is probably my most useful tool in managing her behaviour, keeping her engaged and helping her to learn so it makes sense that it personal tutorials are one of the most important sessions on her timetable.

ADDRESSING EMOTIONAL WELL-BEING FOR CHILDREN WITH PDA IN MAINSTREAM SCHOOLS

There are many children with significant emotional needs attending mainstream schools. A number of these are children with PDA. There is an increasing range of materials available to schools to help them support the emotional well-being of their pupils. Despite the large numbers of pupils at mainstream schools, there are some straightforward systems which most schools can consider to address the needs for their pupils with PDA.

The model of *personal tutorials* which is described in this chapter can be adapted to a range of settings. It requires school leaders who have a sustained commitment to prioritising this area of work. It also requires staff with suitable skills who can work directly with the children. Many schools have pastoral care teams, special needs support staff, mentors and staff who have responsibility for behaviour or well-being. These groups of staff may be a useful place to start if a school is thinking of setting up a system of personal tutorials for some of its pupils. Children in mainstream schools have very full and busy timetables, but tutorials do not need to impact on their curriculum learning. Some schools are able to look creatively at a different use of assembly time, lunch times or the first and last half hours of the school day.

Some schools have found it more practical to set up regular *'check-in' sessions* with pupils. That is when a nominated and trusted member of staff meets, maybe only for 15 minutes, with a pupil at the start and end of each school day. The purpose of these meetings is a more personalised version of the secondary school model of morning tutor time. This is time to check how the pupil is feeling that day, whether they are prepared for any particular events or changes the day will bring, to consider any problem-solving strategies which may be needed and to pick up any social and emotional well-being issues. If an issue arises which requires more time or attention than these brief meetings can provide, then an extra session can be set aside. Working in this way not only helps children feel more supported but contributes to an ongoing relationship of trust between staff and pupil, and provides a way of tackling issues more proactively.

School staff are encouraged to be 'reflective practitioners'. That is to say, they are encouraged as a marker of good practice, to reflect on what they do, how they do it, and how effective they are. By doing so, schools can also look at what they do both with and for their pupils with PDA, what is working well and what is working less well. It can be helpful to examine the styles of those staff who work well with children with PDA, particularly in secondary schools where pupils come across many different teachers with different teaching styles. Once staff become aware of what characterises this beneficial style, it can be looked for and encouraged in other staff.

Mainstream schools can also look at how some of the systems they already have in place can be adapted to meet additional needs of pupils like those with PDA. Useful questions for schools to ask themselves may include:

- Do pupils know where/who they can go to when they are in difficulty? Are these places/people suitable to their individual needs?

- Do we need to look again at how we include and prepare pupils for school trips or special events in school?

- What are these pupils doing at lunchtimes? Is this a slot of the day where we could be giving them more support or social opportunities?

- Can we give these children a role or responsibility within school which will build their self-esteem?

- Can we provide a system of 'emergency exits' for pupils whose anxiety levels have become unmanageable? If so, what do we need to do and how can we support the pupils at these times?

- How effectively are we communicating with and supporting families of children with delicate emotional issues and difficult behaviour?

- Who is overseeing pupil well-being? Will this include well-being for this more complex group of pupils too?

- How do we train and supervise school staff working in this way?

DEVELOPING SELF-AWARENESS IN CHILDREN WITH PDA

Self-awareness is a key skill underlying feelings of security. If we can understand what we feel, why we feel that way and what helps us to feel better, we are in a position to protect ourselves from unnecessary conflict and emotional damage. This is often referred to as 'emotional resilience'. It is also an important long-term skill needed for developing the ability to access appropriate help, make suitable personalised life choices, and to interpret and predict emotional situations.

Some children with PDA will develop a sense of their own differences from quite an early age, while others will find that this comes later; some may find it hard to accept that they have any difficulties at all. Achieving a degree of self-awareness is an important part of maturing as an individual and has a big impact on the life choices young people go on to make. For example, choosing a hobby or a place to live which reflects a realistic view of preferences and abilities will obviously have more positive outcomes. This process is as much about recognising personal skills and aptitudes as well as any limitations. Thorough and beneficial self-awareness is long-term work, however.

At some point, many children with PDA will ask questions about themselves and may refer to their diagnosis. Talking to children about this can be difficult for parents and professionals. The first step, of course, is recognising PDA and building knowledge about it in adults. Understanding and explaining PDA is complex enough for those of us who have lived or worked with it for many years. Trying to explain it in a meaningful and useful way to young people with PDA themselves is even more challenging. It can open up some delicate and complicated conversations but, if it is done sensitively, it can be very valuable in helping young people increase their self-awareness as well as their self-esteem.

Talking to young people about their condition can raise as many questions as answers and should not be undertaken lightly. To be most helpful to the young person, though, it should ideally be done in a planned, collaborative way involving a range of adults who are supporting the child and their family.

The following questions form the basis of frequent discussions with families on this subject:

- Why should adults talk to young people about their condition?

- What should be considered before starting to talk about PDA with a young person?

- What terminology should be used?

- How can PDA be described to a child or young person?

The answers will need to be highly individualised. Plus in most cases, it is families, not professionals, who should take the lead regarding whether to tell their child. Professionals have a role in supporting and guiding the process regarding how to do so.

Why should adults talk to young people about their condition?

Although young people with PDA may have difficulty developing self-awareness, and may sometimes be resistant to the idea that they have additional needs, this is not a reason to avoid guiding them towards a better understanding of themselves. It will, on the other hand, have an influence on *how* these discussions are worked through with them.

Deciding not to talk to children about their condition is of course always an option, but it is an option which has its own consequences. Some young people themselves may have formed their own ideas about their differences and may have come to wrong conclusions, including thinking that their difficulties are someone's fault, or that there are not other people like them. If children are not spoken to about their condition, the risk also increases of them finding out 'accidentally'. This may then push a family into discussions at a time that they would not otherwise have chosen.

There is of course a possibility that once they find out, children may have a negative reaction, or may try to use their PDA as a reason why they are not able to co-operate! These are not uncommon initial reactions, but can be worked through and do not prevent long-term benefits.

What should be considered before starting to talk about PDA with a young person?

The answers to some of the following questions will form the basis of how and where to start the conversations with the young person. They will open up discussion among the people who know the child best and who are involved in supporting them and their family. This can then lead into a co-ordinated and collaborative plan.

- What is their current self-awareness? How would they describe themselves? Are they aware of their own strengths or weaknesses?

- Could their everyday life be improved in the long term if they understood more about their condition?

- How would other people describe them? Is the child or young person aware of how others may perceive them?

- Have they begun to show an awareness of any differences between themselves and their peers?

- If so, in what ways have they expressed this awareness?

- Do they know anything about any additional needs (their own or other people's)?

- What are their strengths and interests (i.e. what strategies or styles will help support them)?

- What do the family and the supporting staff at school think about it?

What terminology should be used?

At the time of writing there is very little literature published about PDA. There is, however, a considerable bank of resources which support explaining the diagnosis of autism and Asperger's syndrome to young people. Although there are of course many key differences between autism and PDA, there are enough similarities to make it possible to use autism as a springboard. Autism spectrum is also currently better known to the general public than PDA. For these reasons, it is probably more useful to the child, to explain their condition as 'a form of autism'. This can then be expanded and individualised such as, 'a form of autism which means that you find it more difficult than most people to manage your anxiety/to co-operate with requests/to make and keep friends', etc. It is significant to refer to the spectrum of autism as meaning that although there are lots of people who can be described as being on that spectrum, they are all affected in their own individual way. They are affected by *their* form of autism or *their* PDA.

How can PDA be described to a child or young person?

There are two strands to this. One is about the *content* of the explanation of the concepts. The other is about the *methods* used to explain.

CONTENT

In terms of the *content*, it can be useful to begin with an exploration of strengths and difficulties, on the understanding that we all have strengths as well as areas of difficulty. It is essential to get as clear a picture as possible of what sense this youngster is already making of himself, his relationships and his environment. This will help adults who support the child to move forward at the right pace and level.

There are some central messages which may be helpful in developing an understanding of what their differences mean to them. These include the following:

- It is likely to be useful and meaningful to describe differences and difficulties in terms of brain function or wiring. Most people's brains function in one way, yours functions in another, which is why you may have noticed that there are some differences between yourself and other children. There are lots of other children whose brains work in a similar way to yours, and there is a special name for people who fall into this group. There is not a better or worse type of brain to have, just different.

- It is not possible to swap your brain. The brain you were born with is the one you will keep all your life. This means that it is not anyone's choice or fault what sort of brain they have. It also means that everyone's brain is unique. That means that whatever sort of person you are, whatever condition you have, will affect you in an equally unique way.

- It can be a good idea for all of us to understand what sort of people we are so that we can get the help we need throughout life. It will also help us to make good choices in terms of relationships, where to live, jobs, hobbies, etc.

- Everyone has difficulty with some things. The impact of these things can change over time and can depend on different circumstances. As you grow up and understand yourself better, the impact of things which challenge you may reduce because you can develop better ways of handling them.

- Understanding more about ourselves is an important part of growing up. You may be at the start of this process. It is a long process and will continue for the rest of your adult life. Everyone has to go through this. There are people around you who understand you and who are able to help you.

- The condition is not visible. This means that there are some people who do know about it but others who do not. People you come across will not be able to 'see' that you have PDA. As you grow up, you may need to make careful choices about who you tell and who you do not. Useful people to tell are people who can help. It may be a good idea to talk to someone who knows you well about whether or not to tell a new person.

- It is OK to be who you are. You are doing really well at being yourself. Being who you are may mean that you have some additional needs. Everyone needs extra help with some things. It can be really helpful if you can identify some useful strategies so that you can build them into your life. It can be useful if you can let other people who support you know what you think you need too. This is true for everyone, so sometimes it is important to respect that other people are doing the best they can at being themselves. This means that sometimes you need to accept that they are using their own strategies, which may be different from yours.

The above points cover some of the underlying tone and content for discussions. Time may need to be spent exploring the core diagnostic features, some of which overlap with autism spectrum disorders. In terms of PDA, it is worth spending extra time on issues of anxiety since this is so often the underlying cause of much demand-avoidant behaviour. It can be more effective to explain the additional needs of someone with PDA in terms of the need to reduce anxiety about demands, rather than in terms of their commitment to avoiding demands. Offering children with PDA a diagnosable reason why they are unable to co-operate could backfire!

As well as talking about what PDA is, it can also be important to talk about what it is not. For instance, some youngsters may have noticed their family use 'disabled' parking and may become anxious that their condition is physical or that they will need to use a wheelchair in the future.

This is the 'grown up Dylan'. Dylan hopes to drive a BMW, have his own flat, learn how to cook, and possibly be a journalist, policeman, or expert on dinosaurs.

It has been useful to other youngsters to point out that it is not an illness, even though they may regularly see a doctor, and that it does not mean that they cannot be ambitious or live a purposeful and satisfying adult life.

METHODS

In terms of the *methods* used to explain the concepts, it is vital to think flexibly about how to time and pace these conversations and how to use a child's personal preferences or interests to engage them.

It can be very helpful to use visual approaches to support these conversations about very personal and conceptual themes. Partly, and in a similar way to other youngsters on the spectrum, this adds clarity and structure. More specifically to children with PDA, using writing, pictures or drawing can de-personalise the perceived demand of the activity, which can increase the chances of co-operation.

It is also important to think about *how* these topics of conversation are opened and sustained with youngsters with PDA. In particular, how their tone can avoid triggering demand avoidance and remain supportive, accepting and non-threatening. Rather than asking closed questions, it is likely to be more effective to use a more open line of questioning. For instance, 'When I talked about people being different, you looked like you were thinking about something really interesting. I wonder if I can guess what it is. Let's play 20 questions', or 'Tell me about your ideal plans for when you're an adult.'

These examples use direct but open questions. Another technique can be to use indirect opening lines, such as 'I know someone who finds it really hard to use their glasses to read because they don't like to think they need help. Everyone needs help with some things, even you and me…'

Some young people with PDA need plenty of opportunities for pauses and breaks to allow for going way off subject before coming back. Equally, children need to have time to talk when it suits them, which does not always coincide with when it suits adults. In these cases, adults can question whether they can in fact be flexible enough to create some time straight away, or whether they can make an arrangement *with the child* to do so at another time. Similarly, if an adult has set aside some time to explore some of these issues and the moment does not actually feel right for the child, the adult can 'set the scene' as far as is reasonable, but then needs to postpone the conversation.

Wider considerations

Once adults have started to have conversations with a child which are building towards their understanding of their differences, there are some other wider implications to think about. Aside from thinking about who will talk to them and what they will actually say, it is helpful to also think about some of the following points:

- When and where will they have opportunities for regular conversations?

- Who supports the rest of the family, including siblings?

- How will other people involved in working and living with the child be kept informed of what they have discussed and what sense the child has made of it?

- Are there other people in the child's wider circle who need to know that these discussions have been opened up (e.g. babysitters, grandparents)? These people do not need to be involved in progressing the discussions but may well benefit from at least knowing that they have begun.

CONCLUDING REMARKS

This chapter has explored some examples of encouraging emotional understanding and self-awareness in children with PDA. Working through some of these issues can present challenges to children with PDA as well as to the adults who support them. Adults who do well at this will have developed a fine balance between style and content which is characterised by:

- prioritising a secure and trusting relationship between adult and child to underpin work on more sensitive and emotional issues

- individualised approaches which build on interests

- well-paced interactions which gauge the balance between demands made and the child's tolerance at a given moment

- collaborative attitudes to including families and other professionals involved with a child

- the use of attitudes in the adults which are accepting, empathetic, good-humoured, non-judgemental and patient

- the use of skills on the part of adults which are flexible, non-directive and reflective.

It is crucial to the success of interacting with children with PDA that adults develop their understanding not only of the child and the condition, but also of themselves and the contribution that they make to the relationship or conversation. Children with PDA can be as engaging as they can be exhausting. They require adults who support them to be flexible, appealing, creative and calm. This means that adults need to work supportively and collaboratively with each other, with the children and with their families. These comments are true for effectively supporting children with PDA in every context. They are particularly important regarding the longer-term perspective of helping children develop their self-awareness, emotional resilience and the skills to manage their own behaviour. These are crucial elements to ensuring better outcomes as children leave school and enter adulthood. Some of the issues which may arise beyond the school years are outlined in Chapter 6.

Chapter 6

SUMMING UP AND QUESTIONS FOR THE FUTURE

INTRODUCTION

This book is primarily aimed at parents and those professionals who come into day-to-day contact with children with PDA and their families. It is also intended to be relevant to those working in health, social care and education who may support children and families in different ways. It brings together what is currently known about PDA from a research, clinical and educational perspective. These understandings have been illustrated by the insights and views of parents trying to deal with their own experience of bringing up a child with PDA within their family, at the same time as dealing with services which often don't recognise, understand or provide effectively for their needs. The text has been supplemented by many individual examples and descriptions of practice, which we hope provide useful insights, suggestions and strategies.

This is the first book published about PDA, some 30 years or so after the first clinical accounts were written by Elizabeth Newson. This is a similar period of time between Kanner's first descriptions of autism, in 1943, and the early publications on clinical and educational aspects of autism in the UK (J.K. Wing 1966; M. Rutter 1971; L. Wing 1971). In one of these, *Autistic Children: A Guide for Parents* by Lorna Wing, the sleeve notes reported 'a recent survey has shown that there are some 6,000 autistic children in Great Britain alone'. Today, a further 30 years later, the National

Autistic Society website suggests that there are half a million people with autism in the UK. This is based on a review of prevalence studies throughout the UK since 1966, which suggests a 'best fit' prevalence rate of 1 in 100 children with an autism spectrum disorder. This is broadly equivalent to the estimate of autism prevalence in the US of 1 in 110, reported by the Centers for Disease Control in 2009. The debate continues about how much, if any, of this increase is a result of unexplained environmental factors and their interaction with genetic susceptibility. It certainly and dramatically demonstrates how much our understanding of autism has changed and developed over this time, particularly with the concept of the 'spectrum' of autism that has broadened the category and increased the numbers of children diagnosed. Alongside increased recognition and changing definitions, there has been an increase in our knowledge about approaches and interventions and the services that people with autism and their families require.

As far as PDA is concerned, we are of course still at a very early stage of understanding its true nature and extent, how it relates to other conditions and where it lies within the autism spectrum. The accounts and descriptions of PDA that have been published, though, bring about a strong sense of recognition and resonate with the experiences of many professionals and parents. These descriptions, and the explanations put forward so far, have also been enormously helpful to many parents, teachers and others looking for a better understanding of particular children and ways in which they might relate to them more effectively. There is, however, much more that needs to be done to improve our knowledge and develop ways of providing more effective support.

IMPROVING AWARENESS, RECOGNITION AND UNDERSTANDING OF PDA

As this book was being completed, early in 2011, the first major national conference on PDA took place in London, organised by the National Autistic Society (NAS) in association with NORSACA. The response to the event was remarkable with over 400 attending from all over the UK. Delegates included professionals from health, education and social care as well as many parents, all wanting to improve their understanding of the condition. Details of the event, copies of presentations and videos can all be found on the conferences section of the NAS website.

At the end of the conference, delegates were asked to complete a short survey which asked what were the most important areas for development in relation to our knowledge about PDA. Among professionals, the most urgent priority was seen to be supplementing the clinical and educational accounts that have been written with further evidence from empirical research. This was the focus of one of the presentations, entitled 'New Research Ideas and Questions about PDA', given by Francesca Happé (Professor of Cognitive Neuroscience) and Liz O'Nions (postgraduate research student) of the Social, Genetic and Developmental Psychiatry Centre, Institute of Psychiatry, King's College, London. The first part of the presentation underlined the fact that PDA was much discussed and described but little researched. It also outlined the type of evidence base that would be needed for PDA to be considered for entry into the diagnostic manuals. They went on to describe the new research that has taken place and is planned at the SGDP centre. We are grateful for them for allowing a summary of this to be included here.

CURRENT AND PLANNED RESEARCH ON PDA AT THE INSTITUTE OF PSYCHIATRY, KING'S COLLEGE, LONDON

Exploring the behavioural profile in PDA

To date, a questionnaire study has taken place to describe the behavioural profile in PDA, prior to embarking on projects to examine what is driving behaviour. The questionnaire study looked at the behavioural profile in 40 children with PDA aged 9–16, in terms of parent reported autistic like traits, social interaction problems, difficult behaviour and anxiety (O'Nions *et al.* in preparation).

The new data collected from parents of children with PDA was compared to data from over 5000 12-year-old children from an existing database of children representative of the general population.

This allowed an examination of the severity of problems experienced by children with PDA, determining where on the population distribution of scores they fall on each measure.

Within the large population sample, 39 children had an ASD diagnosis, and 28 had very high levels of 'conduct problems', behaviours associated with 'oppositional-defiant disorder' (ODD) and 'conduct disorder' (CD) such as impulsivity, aggression, and a tendency to lie or cheat. This enabled comparisons to be made between three clinical groups: children with PDA, those with ASD and others with conduct problems (CP).

The study showed that children with PDA resemble those with ASD on questionnaire measures of *autistic like traits* and social interaction problems. Items where the PDA group scored more strongly than the ASD group included 'has difficulty understanding the rules for polite behaviour', 'turns conversations around to what they want to discuss' and 'imposes routines on themselves and others'. It was also noted that, as described in earlier clinical descriptions, children with PDA were reported to have better eye-contact and conversational skills than children with ASD.

When comparing the three clinical groups on items reflecting *difficulties with social interaction*, children with PDA (like those with autism) were in the one per cent of the population that has most difficulties with social interaction. The difficulties children with PDA were reported to have with social interaction differentiated them from the group of children with conduct problems and indicates that PDA is not just another term used to describe children with these sorts of behavioural difficulties.

When the PDA group was compared to children with conduct problems in relation to *difficult behaviour* (e.g. impulsivity, temper tantrums and poor planning) both groups scored in the one per cent of the population showing the most difficult behaviour.

Looking at these comparisons it might be tempting to conclude that PDA should be viewed as a 'double hit': an ASD together with personality traits associated with conduct problems. However, the

PDA group had higher levels of *parent-rated anxiety* than both the ASD and CP groups and were in the two per cent of the population sample with the highest level of anxiety.

Future research directions in PDA

While the findings presented above suggest there is behavioural overlap between PDA and both ASD and CP, research is needed to examine whether there is continuity between these disorders at the genetic, neural and cognitive levels. The next step is to focus on 'cognitive continuity'.

To illustrate what is meant by this, recent research into autism spectrum disorders has shown that children with autism do not spontaneously see things from others' points of view, something that for typically developing individuals is so intuitive that it requires no effort (Baron-Cohen, Leslie and Frith 1985). For example, if you walk into a room and someone in there is furtively tucking a book behind the sofa, you intuit that they do not want you to see the book.

The failure of this intuition in ASD is sometimes described as impaired 'theory of mind'. It means that individuals with autism have great difficulty deceiving others, as to do this requires being able to predict what someone will think if you tell them a lie. In addition, they can also have great difficulty understanding their own thoughts and feelings.

Understanding what is causing the difficulties associated with ASD at the cognitive level has proved extremely helpful for parents and teachers, who can better understand their child's difficulties. For example, a student who frequently corrects their teacher's spelling in class is not trying to embarrass the teacher, but just can't see that this might be upsetting from the teacher's point of view.

Understanding the causes of PDA at the cognitive level is a major aim for the research. One of the research questions that will be explored is whether children with PDA have difficulty with theory of mind, though their ability to distract, trick or divert seems to suggest not. If theory of mind is not implicated in PDA, other avenues will involve exploring emotion processing, empathy or emotional detachment, and a sense of their own identity.

Other hypotheses may come from exploring why typically developing children do comply so readily, to better understand why children with PDA refuse to. Some tentative hypotheses are that typically developing children have (but perhaps lacking in PDA) a need to please others, a fear of being rejected by them, a herd instinct, or a need to maintain their social standing and reputation.

Identifying PDA: Developing assessment tools

Developing tools to identify PDA is important for both research and clinical purposes. There are many established questionnaires that quantify the severity of behaviours characteristic of other disorders, (e.g. the Childhood Asperger Syndrome Test: Scott *et al.* 2002). Questionnaires are also useful to clinicians when acquiring information to make diagnostic or referral decisions in a systematic manner.

During the research, in consultation with clinicians, *a new parent report questionnaire for PDA* has been established. This is only the second instrument developed to measure PDA, the other being the Diagnostic Interview for Social and Communication Disorders (DISCO) (L. Wing *et al.* 2002) which contains 17 items targeting PDA-related behaviours.

It is important to test whether the questionnaire is capable of distinguishing individuals with PDA from those with other disorders. This will involve distributing copies of the questionnaire to parents of children aged 6–17 who either have PDA, are 'typically developing', or have another diagnosis, or suspected diagnoses. This will demonstrate whether the questionnaire can differentiate diagnosed PDA from these other groups. Once the questionnaire has been validated, it will be useful as a screening tool for clinicians and researchers.

A second strand of work, aiming to improve identification of PDA, is to develop *an observational schedule* for use during clinical interviews/play assessments. Currently, observation schedules including the

Autism Diagnostic Observation Schedule-ADOS (Lord *et al.* 1989) are used by clinicians to diagnose ASD. The ADOS is a structured tool that involves a series of tasks such as making up a story with toy figures, as well as free conversation. At the end, the assessor makes ratings of various aspects of the child's behaviour reflecting the domains associated with ASD.

It is planned to develop some question items to measure PDA-related behaviours that occur during clinical or play-based assessments. These might reflect, for example, whether the child wants to be in control of the session, or spontaneously slips into role when asked to do something. In addition, some additional tasks, or probe questions, will be generated which are designed to measure theory of mind, pro-sociality, desire to manage their reputation, and empathy, which could be incorporated into an assessment.

Research-based evidence such as this is critical in supporting the clinical understandings about PDA that have developed. It will help to establish more certainty and consensus about the characteristics that typify children with PDA and improve reliability in distinguishing them from children with other conditions. It will also deepen our understanding of the key differences in social and emotional understanding that seem to be at the heart of PDA and which lead to the anxiety-driven need to be in control and the demand avoidance that has been described.

While awareness, recognition and understanding of the condition is growing, the experience of parents is very variable, according to where they live and the particular professionals that they come into contact with. Both the Elizabeth Newson Centre and the PDA Contact Group are frequently asked by parents if there are any professionals in their area who recognise PDA and are able, or willing, to make a diagnosis. At one time the number of professionals using the term was very limited, and many of those who raised the possibility of PDA as an appropriate description would want to refer the child to Nottingham for the diagnosis to be 'confirmed'. This still happens in some cases in areas where there is awareness of the condition but lack of confidence on the part of local paediatricians, psychologists or psychiatrists. There are, though, an increasing number of professionals who recognise the profile, see the description as a useful explanation and are confident in making the diagnosis.

At the London conference Dr Judy Gould (Director of the NAS Lorna Wing Centre) discussed the Diagnostic Interview for Social and Communication Disorders (DISCO), which is used as part of the diagnostic process. The DISCO has over 500 questions relating to development and untypical behaviours. Within this there are 17 questions related to PDA, based on the original descriptions by Elizabeth Newson. These include descriptions of behaviour such as: 'lacks awareness of age group, social hierarchy etc.' and 'socially manipulative behaviour to avoid demands'. Dr Gould pointed out that features of PDA can be found in children and young people across the autism spectrum, but where they cluster together they represent the PDA profile. She went on to conclude that 'diagnostically the PDA sub-group is recognisable and has implications for management and support'. Dr Gould, in conjunction with Dr Jacqui Ashton-Smith (Principal, Helen Allison School), also reflected on the gender bias within the diagnosis of autism spectrum disorders contrasting the commonly accepted boy to girl ratio of 4:1 in autism and 12:1 in Asperger's syndrome with the equal number of boys and girls with PDA, as described by Elizabeth Newson. A high proportion of the traits shared by girls on the autism spectrum are those traits related to PDA. Further work in this fascinating area of gender difference within the spectrum may well also add to our understanding of PDA.

Another presentation was given by Dr Jacqueline Morgan (Associate Specialist in Neuro-developmental Paediatrics) and Dr Natalie Roberts (clinical psychologist) who are members of the Specialist Child and Adolescent Mental Health Service (CAMHS) teams in Winchester and Andover, Hampshire. They gave an account of their 'journey' to respond to the needs of children with PDA and their families across the county. Early on in this process there had been contact with the Elizabeth Newson Centre in connection with individual referrals, training and discussion, which led to adaptations of their own assessment process and history taking which informed their own use of the diagnosis. This led to further developments, such as the formation of a parent support group and, crucially, the provision of training at the request of the County Autism Group. This helped to secure the involvement of education professionals who were increasingly recognising that children with this diagnosis had particular support needs. More recently, in response to the increasing numbers of children within the county receiving the diagnosis, a meeting was arranged which led to the formation of the multi-agency Test Valley PDA Working Group. Multi-agency working such as this would, if it were repeated in other areas of the country, vastly improve the consistency of service offered to children with PDA and their families.

IMPROVING PROVISION AND SUPPORT

If a child is diagnosed earlier, and appropriate support provided sooner, parents and others are likely to become better at understanding, managing and communicating with the child. In Chapter 4 it was acknowledged that there is little research evidence about the relative benefits of different educational placements and about which children benefit most from specialist or mainstream placements. It is also the case that, in the field of ASDs generally, attempts to evaluate different types of intervention, or approaches, used with children on the autism spectrum have been fraught with difficulties. These include defining what a successful 'outcome' is for a particular child, understanding which changes in a child's development can be attributed to the particular intervention and which to other factors, as well knowing what the outcome might have been if the child hadn't received the intervention in the first place.

Anecdotally one of the clearest messages that we receive from parents and teachers is that children with PDA do not typically respond well to the more conventional approaches that are so effective for children with other ASDs. They also tell us, though, that the type of approach detailed in Chapter 2, and previously outlined in Elizabeth Newson's 'handling guidelines', can make a real difference.

A parent wrote about her son, Marcus:

I couldn't understand why on Monday I could ask Marcus to put his shoes on and he might do it but on Tuesday he would scream, shout, hit and kick me until I had to carry him to the car and put the shoes on in the car afterwards! Marcus can tell me he loves me and literally ten seconds later tells me he hates me. He can be tickling me one minute and thumping me the next – he is very volatile. I think this is the most difficult aspect of my son's behaviour. Years of trying to manage his behaviour with strategies for autism had left me confused, frustrated, disillusioned, and feeling like I had given birth to the devil's son! I knew that my son's autism diagnosis wasn't quite right.

After reading the criteria for PDA I just knew it was the right diagnosis for my son. I said, 'Yes. At last, this is what he has!' As I read up everything I could about it and started to use the indirect methods of behaviour management our lives became more manageable. At least now I can sometimes understand what will cause Marcus to have a meltdown. You cannot make PDA go away but you have to accept it in your child and work hard to manage their behaviours.

The developments in Hampshire that were described earlier led to a working group focusing on the purpose of diagnosis as being to 'better understand and make sense of a child and use that understanding to formulate more effective forms of intervention and provision'. The group is currently refining a set of draft guidelines for use throughout the county to co-ordinate local training opportunities and identify successful practice locally, both within schools as a whole and in individual practitioners.

It would be helpful now to identify and describe examples of good practice in a wider and more systematic way. This could involve provision in both mainstream and special schools, looking at practice at both whole-school and classroom levels and across the age ranges. This would provide an opportunity to look at commonality and differences between various provisions and continue the development of good practice guidelines.

Chapter 3 outlined many of the issues faced by families bringing up a child with PDA, both practical and emotional. Children on the autism spectrum often show more challenging behaviour than children with other types of additional needs, and their parents and siblings may have higher levels of stress. Parents frequently feel that the needs of their child and the demands that they place on them as a family aren't fully recognised, particularly when the child has comparatively good expressive language. This is especially the case for parents of children with PDA, who are less likely to have their needs understood and more likely to face misinterpretation of their child's condition from both professionals and others. Within the conference survey one parent commented: 'Because of his ability and social manipulation, people fail to appreciate just how exhausting he is, and how much of an impact he has on family life. Respite needs are therefore not seen as a priority for us by others.'

For some parents the behaviours shown by their child can be extremely distressing and stressful to live with. In addition, there is a need for a much higher level of supervision and attention than with another child of a similar age. There may also be safety issues, which means that it is hard for parents to have time on their own. Practical issues are most often compounded by anxieties about how best to manage their child, concerns about them while they are in school and worries for the future. The PDA Contact Group has been an invaluable source of support and information for many families and a few local support groups have also been set up. Advice lines and family support services, such as those operated by the NAS, NORSACA and other voluntary groups, report an increasing number of calls from families of children with PDA. There is a need to develop the knowledge and understanding of these workers about the distinctive needs of children with PDA to enable them to provide the best possible support. Linsey Atkins the Principal Family Services Worker at NORSACA made the following comments about the way in which her team aims to support families by developing their understanding of the condition:

In learning more about what 'drives' their child's PDA parents realise that a central theme of *control* is ever present. The compulsive need to use avoidance is the interplay between the child or young person's need to control, and their anxiety and stress at losing this control. Once an understanding of PDA and the principles for management have been 'embedded', situations can become easier to predict, strategies can be worked out in advance. Direct confrontation can be redirected with 'softer' requests, offering where possible alternative choices for the young person so they still maintain some control of those situations.

For parents and carers, 'finger tip' strategies need to be well practised and rehearsed – getting ahead of the situation is vital – predicting how the person is likely to react will give parents a better chance of managing it more positively.

In accepting that the child cannot cope well with the demands that are placed on them, this may mean an attitudinal change for the parent or carer which can make family life tolerable again. Understanding that 'head-on' confrontations will not positively achieve what they want, parents often need permission to 'back down'. It challenges our usual concept of being a parent (ensuring we steer our offspring on the right course) but with understanding that personal safety and preservation need to be balanced to maintain some semblance of family life.

MOVING INTO ADULTHOOD – WHAT IS THE OUTLOOK?

There is a need to gather more information about children with PDA as they grow into adulthood so that we can better understand some of the issues that face them at this time of transition. One way of doing this is through contact with individuals, families and schools over extended periods of time in the form of longitudinal studies. It would also be useful to know more about the views and experiences of individuals with the condition themselves. The literature about autism and Asperger's syndrome has been greatly enhanced by the growing number of autobiographical accounts. Much of this has also informed our understandings of the way in which we relate to, and work with, children and young people on the spectrum. For example, it has increased our appreciation of sensory differences and encouraged us to take more account of the views and preferences of each individual.

Elizabeth Newson and Claire David (1999) did carry out a survey following up a sample of 18 individuals aged 16 or over who had an earlier diagnosis of PDA. Fifteen of these were between the ages of 16 and 24 at the time of the survey. The main purpose of the study was to ask how robust the diagnostic pattern of PDA was over time within each individual. As well as asking questions, through a parental questionnaire, about diagnostic characteristics, information was also gathered about educational and social history, employment and hopes for the future. Newson and David found that the features that characterise the PDA profile were persistent and endured over time. All but one individual was described as still 'obsessively resistant', but seven young people were seen as less avoidant than formerly. The continuing problems with impulsivity and mood swings affected all but one individual, with most still becoming violent when angry. This, alongside difficulties in social and emotional understanding, meant that many had got into trouble as young adults in one way or another. A number had been in trouble with the police, but the majority not charged. For some of those who had been in trouble this was based around their fascination with specific people. When parents were asked about 'obsessional behaviour', 12 of the young people were said to show this focus on particular individuals, either blaming or targeting specific people in some way. All but two were felt by their parents to be easily led and 'set up' and were said to be 'sexually vulnerable'.

As far as their education experience and attainments were concerned, parents, unsurprisingly, reported that a high level of individual support had been essential in maintaining their school placement. It was pointed out, though, that often this provision was reactive, arriving after an episode of failure. In line with what was said in Chapter 4, 13 of the children had experienced exclusion, or breakdown of placement, and for several this occurred a number of times, with one girl being excluded from seven different placements. Educational attainments were very disappointing, and Newson contrasted this with the attainments of those with Asperger's syndrome. Only one participant in the study achieved GCSE standard, although another young person declined participation in the study saying that she was at university abroad following very good support throughout school. In a smaller sample of six, carried out by Andrea Robinson in a student research project in 2007, the picture was more positive in this respect and three out of the six attained GCSE standard with one of these going on to university. The majority of young people in the original study were in some form of special education college (either day or residential), most with enhanced support. Parents of children in both groups understandably expressed fears for the future in relation to their child's ability to live independently and gain any form of employment, and about what would happen to their son or daughter if they were no longer able to provide care, and of their social vulnerability and risk.

It would be especially valuable to repeat this sort of study with a larger sample, giving more of a focus to suggestions, and examples of practice, that have proved useful in supporting young people with PDA growing up and dealing with some of these issues. A number of parents in the conference survey emphasised the need for more strategies and information about dealing with issues around sex and relationships and 'independence vs. vulnerability'. There has been very little, if anything, written about this in relation to PDA, but some of the material developed for young people with other ASDs might be a useful starting point. One practical and accessible resource is 'Sex & Relationship Education: A Programme for Learners with Autistic Spectrum Disorders' by Fiona Speirs (www.fionaspeirs.co.uk), which covers modules that include the physical self, sexual expressions, life choices and staying safe.

Many parents have found the information reported in the outcome study as very discouraging and pessimistic. It should be remembered, though, that the group of young people included may not have been fully representative of the condition as a whole. By being known to the Elizabeth Newson Centre in the first place it is likely that they were mostly young people with more significant needs. It must also be remembered that these children were mainly diagnosed quite late on and at a time when very little was known, or understood, about some of the teaching and management approaches that are proving more effective.

At the same time, individuals with PDA and their families will need support throughout their lives. Parents' fears for the future mirror those of parents of children with other ASDs, but may be magnified by the variable recognition and understanding of the condition and some of the particular challenges in behaviour that persist for some young people with PDA. Parents express worries about their children's needs, about 'falling through the net' of those services provided for people with learning disabilities and mental health, about them getting into trouble with the criminal justice system, about not having enough support to live independently, about the demands placed on them and other family members as carers, and about what will happen to their son or daughter when they are no longer able to provide them with support.

Research carried out by the National Autistic Society (Rosenblatt 2008) found that 63 per cent of adults on the autism spectrum do not have enough support to meet their needs and as a result 61 per cent rely on their families for financial support, with over 45 per cent living with their parents and only 15 per cent in full-time employment. Over 90 per cent of parents were said to be worried, or very worried, about their son or daughter's future when they are no longer able to support them. The same research reported that 98 per cent of local authorities and 100 per cent of primary care trusts want more support to deliver services for adults on the autism spectrum. This research study formed part of the NAS response to the consultation process leading up to the drafting of the Autism Act 2009. This act made key provisions which required the government to produce an adult autism strategy by April 2010 and that statutory guidance be issued for local authorities and health bodies on supporting the needs of adults with autism (*Fulfilling and Rewarding Lives: The Strategy for Adults with Autism in England*: Department of Health 2010). This guidance sends a clear message to local councils and health bodies that they must improve training for staff, identification and diagnosis in adults, planning of services and local leadership. It is clearly the intention of this guidance to improve significantly the way that services are delivered for all adults on the autism spectrum. Within this it should also improve some of the experiences and opportunities for people with PDA, and underline the need for the condition to be recognised, identified and understood as being part of the autism spectrum.

CONCLUDING COMMENTS

In writing this book we have been especially conscious of wanting to strike a balance between describing the enormous difficulties experienced by many children and families, while at the same time giving positive examples of practice and ways in which children can be effectively supported. PDA, like other conditions within the autism spectrum, is a life-long condition that can have enormous impact on the opportunities of the person affected and cause massive problems for the family, both practically and emotionally. At the same time, a better understanding of the distinctive profile and needs of children with PDA is gradually emerging and, with it, a greater recognition of which provision and approaches and are most needed and effective. There is an emerging consensus about what the key issues are and what makes sense in the way that children with PDA are best supported. There are examples of good practice developing around the needs of individual children, which are being shared in a way that can have wider benefit. This book has been part of that process. It is hoped that it will generate further discussion, research and dissemination of ideas among both parents and professionals so that they will be better placed to provide appropriate understanding and support in the future.

Appendix 1

USEFUL WEBSITES AND LINKS

Advisory Centre for Education

www.ace-ed.org.uk

A national charity that has been advising parents and carers of children aged 5–16 in state-funded education for 50 years.

Autism Education Trust

www.autismeducationtrust.org.uk

The Autism Education Trust (AET) was launched in November 2007 with funding from the Department for Children, Schools and Families. It is dedicated to co-ordinating and improving education support for all children on the autism spectrum in England.

Cerebra

www.cerebra.org.uk

Cerebra is a unique charity set up to help improve the lives of children with brain-related conditions through researching, educating and directly supporting children and their carers.

National Autistic Society

www.autism.org.uk

The leading UK charity for people with autism (including Asperger's syndrome) and their families. They provide information, support and pioneering services, and campaign for a better world for people with autism.

NORSACA

www.norsaca.org.uk

NORSACA is a charity that enables people with autism to live their lives with dignity, choice and independence. It includes links to the Elizabeth Newson Centre and Sutherland House School.

OAASIS

www.oaasis.co.uk

A resource for parents and professionals caring for children and young people with autism/Asperger's syndrome and other learning disabilities.

Parent Partnership

www.parentpartnership.org.uk

This website provides information about how to find their local Parent Partnership Service.

PDA Contact Group

www.pdacontact.org.uk

A website offering information on PDA and its characteristics.

PDA Contact Group Forum

http://ccgi.pdacontact.org.uk/forum

This is an online forum for parents and professionals to offer each other advice on all aspects of PDA.

Sibs

www.sibs.org.uk

Support for brothers and sisters of those with special needs, disabilities or chronic illness.

Appendix 2

BOOKLIST

The following booklist recommends a selection of publications that may be useful for children with PDA and those who live and work with them. In the absence of much literature specifically written about PDA, many of the resources include 'autism' or 'Asperger's' in their title. This does not mean that they are not appropriate for children and young people with PDA, but that they will need some adaptation.

PICTURE BOOKS TO USE WITH CHILDREN AND YOUNG PEOPLE

(These are story books aimed at primary-aged children.)

Al-Ghani, K.I. and Al-Ghani, H. (2008) *The Red Beast: Controlling Anger in Children with Asperger's Syndrome*. London: Jessica Kingsley Publishers.

Cave, K. and Riddell, C. (1995) *Something Else*. London: Penguin.

Ironside, V. (1996) *The Huge Bag of Worries*. London: Hodder.

Sunderland, M. (2000) *Willy and the Wobbly House*. Bicester: Winslow Press.

Sunderland, M. (2003) *How Hattie Hated Kindness*. Bicester: Winslow Press.

ACTIVITY BOOKS TO USE WITH CHILDREN AND YOUNG PEOPLE

(These are resources which can be personalised and include worksheets.)

Davies, J. (1993) *Children with Pathological Demand Avoidance Syndrome: A Booklet for Brothers and Sisters*. Nottingham: Elizabeth Newson Centre.

Faherty, C. (2000) *Asperger's… What Does It Mean to Me? A Workbook Explaining Self Awareness and Life Lessons to the Child or Youth with High Functioning Autism or Asperger's*. Arlington, TX: Future Horizons.

Huebner, D. (2006) *What to Do When You Worry Too Much – A Kid's Guide to Overcoming Anxiety.* Washington, DC: Magination Press.

Huebner, D. (2007) *What to Do When You Grumble Too Much – A Kid's Guide to Overcoming Negativity.* Washington, DC: Magination Press.

Leventhal-Belfer, L. (2008) *Why Do I Have To? A Book for Children Who Find Themselves Frustrated by Everyday Rules.* London: Jessica Kingsley Publishers.

Plummer, D. (2007) *Helping Children to Build Self-esteem.* London: Jessica Kingsley Publishers.

Simmonds, J. (2003) *Seeing Red – An Anger Management and Peacemaking Curriculum for Kids.* Gabriola Island, BC: New Society Publishers.

Vermeulen, P. (2000) *I Am Special: Introducing Children and Young People to their Autistic Spectrum Disorder.* London: Jessica Kingsley Publishers.

Whitehouse, E. and Pudney, W. (1996) *A Volcano in My Tummy – Helping Children to Handle Anger.* Gabriola Island, BC: New Society Publishers.

BOOKS FOR PARENTS AND PROFESSIONALS

Buron, K.D. (2006) *When My Worries Get Too Big! A Relaxation Book for Children with Autism Spectrum Disorders.* Shawnee Mission, KS: Autism Asperger Publishing.

Buron, K.D. (2007) *A 5 Is Against The Law! Social Boundaries: Straight Up An Honest Guide for Teens and Young Adults.* Shawnee Mission, KS: Autism Asperger Publishing.

Buron, K.D. and Curtis, M. (2003) *The Incredible 5-Point Scale: Assisting Students with Autism Spectrum Disorders in Understanding Social Interactions and Controlling Their Emotional Responses.* Shawnee Mission, KS: Autism Asperger Publishing.

Good Autism Practice: The GAP journal was set up in 2000 to meet the needs of practitioners and parents living or working with individuals on the autism spectrum of all ages. The journal is multi-disciplinary in scope for professionals in services provided by health, social services and education as well as parents and individuals on the autism spectrum. It is published biannually in May and October by BILD (British Institute of Learning Disabilities).

Gray, C. (1994) *Comic Strip Conversations.* Arlington, TX: Future Horizons.

Gray, C. and White, A.L. (2002) *My Social Stories Book.* London: Jessica Kingsley Publishers.

Greene, R.W. (2005) *The Explosive Child.* New York, NY: HarperCollins.

Hobday, A. and Ollier, K. (1998) *Creative Therapy – Activities with Children and Adolescents.* Leicester: BPS Books.

Lipsky, D. and Richards, W. (2009) *Managing Meltdowns.* London: Jessica Kingsley Publishers.

Smith, C. (2003) *Writing and Developing Social Stories.* Bicester: Speechmark Publishing.

Williams, C. and Wright, B. (2004) *How to Live with Autism and Asperger Syndrome: Practical Strategies for Parents and Professionals.* London: Jessica Kingsley Publishers.

REFERENCES

Al-Ghani, K.I. and Al-Ghani, H. (2008) *The Red Beast: Controlling Anger in Children with Asperger's Syndrome*. London: Jessica Kingsley Publishers.

American Psychiatric Association (1994) *Diagnostic and Statistical Manual of Mental Disorders* (4th edn) (DSM-IV) Washington, DC: APA.

Autism Education Trust (2008) *Educational Provision for Children and Young People on the Autism Spectrum Living in England: A Review of Current Practice, Issues and Challenges*. London: Autism Education Trust.

Autism Education Trust (2010) *Tools for Teachers: Practical Strategies for Classroom Success*. London: Autism Education Trust.

Baron-Cohen, S., Leslie, A.M. and Frith, U. (1985) 'Does the autistic child have a Theory of Mind?' *Cognition 21*, 37–46.

Bishop, D. (2003) *Children's Communication Checklist (CCC-2)* (2nd edn). Cambridge: Cambridge University Press.

Buron, K.D. and Curtis, M. (2003) *The Incredible 5-Point Scale: Assisting Students with Autism Spectrum Disorders in Understanding Social Interactions and Controlling Their Emotional Responses*. Shawnee Mission, KS: Autism Asperger Publishing.

Carpenter, B. (2010) *Complex Learning Difficulties and Disabilities*. London: Specialist Schools and Academies Trust.

Centers for Disease Control (2009) 'Prevalence of Autism Spectrum Disorders – Autism and Developmental Disabilities Monitoring Network, United States, 2006.' *Morbidity and Mortality Weekly Report 58* (SS-10).

Christie, P. (2007) 'The distinctive clinical and educational needs of children with Pathological Demand Avoidance syndrome: Guidelines for good practice.' *Good Autism Practice 8*, 1, 3–11.

Christie, P., Fidler, R., Butterfield, B. and Davies, K. (2008) 'Promoting social and emotional development in children with autism: One school's approach.' *Good Autism Practice 9*, 2, 32–38.

Christie, P., Newson, E., Prevezer, W. and Newson, J. (1992) 'An Interactive Approach to Language and Communication for Non-speaking Children.' In D.A. Lane and A. Miller (eds) *Handbook of Child and Adolescent Therapy*. Buckingham: Open University Press.

Christie, P. and Wimpory, D. (1986) 'Recent research into the development of communicative competence: Implications for teaching autistic children.' *Communication 20*, 1, 4–7.

Constructive Campaigning Parent Support Project (2007) *Disobedience or Disability? The Exclusion of Children with Autism from Education*. London: Treehouse.

Davies, J. (1993) *Children with Pathological Demand Avoidance Syndrome: A Booklet for Brothers and Sisters*. Nottingham: Elizabeth Newson Centre.

Davies, J. (1994) *Brothers and Sisters of Children with Autism: A Checklist of Things to Do or Consider for Their Support.* Nottingham: Elizabeth Newson Centre.

Davies, J. and Newson, E. (1994) 'Supporting the Siblings of Children with Autism and Related Developmental Disorders.' In P. Mittler and H. Mittler (eds) *Innovations in Family Support for People with Learning Disabilities.* Chorley: Lisieux Hall.

Department for Children, Schools and Families (2007) *Social and Emotional Aspects of Learning.* London: DCSF.

Department for Children, Schools and Families (2008) *Working Together: Listening to the Voices of Children and Young People.* London: DCSF.

Department for Children, Schools and Families (2009a) *Inclusion Development Programme: Supporting Children on the Autism Spectrum.* London: DCSF.

Department for Children, Schools and Families (2009b) *Special Educational Needs: A Guide for Parents and Carers.* London: DCSF.

Department for Education and Skills (2001) *SEN Code of Practice.* Nottingham: DFES.

Department for Education and Skills (2004) *Every Child Matters.* Nottingham: DFES.

Department for Education and Skills and Department of Health (2002) *Autistic Spectrum Disorders: Good Practice Guidance.* Nottingham: DfES.

Department of Health (2010) *Fulfilling and Rewarding Lives: The Strategy for Adults with Autism in England.* London: DoH.

Faherty, C. (2000) *Asperger's… What Does It Mean to Me? A Workbook Explaining Self Awareness and Life Lessons to the Child or Youth with High Functioning Autism or Asperger's.* Arlington, TX: Future Horizons.

Gray, C. (1994) *Comic Strip Conversations.* Arlington, TX: Future Horizons.

Greene, R.W. (2005) *The Explosive Child.* New York, NY: HarperCollins.

Lamb, B. (2009) *Special Educational Needs and Parental Confidence.* London: DCSF.

Lipsky, D. and Richards, W. (2009) *Managing Meltdowns.* London: Jessica Kingsley Publishers.

Lord, C., Rutter, M., Goode, S., Heemsberger, J. *et al.* (1989) 'Autism diagnostic observation schedule: A standardized observation of communicative and social behavior.' *Journal of Autism and Developmental Disorders 19,* 2, 185–212.

National Autistic Society (2010) *'You Need to Know' Campaign.* London: National Autistic Society.

National Initiative for Autism: Screening and Assessment (2003) *National Autism Plan for Children: Plan for the Identification, Assessment, Diagnosis and Access to Early Interventions for Pre-school Children with Autism Spectrum Disorders.* London: National Autistic Society.

National Institute for Health and Clinical Excellence (2009) *Scope for Consultation on 'Autism Spectrum Disorders in Children and Young People'.* London: NICE.

Newson, E. (1990) *Pathological Demand Avoidance Syndrome: Mapping a New Entity Related to Autism?* Inaugural lecture, University of Nottingham.

Newson, E. (1996) *Pathological Demand Avoidance Syndrome: A Statistical Update in Therapeutic Intervention in Autism: Perspectives from Research and Practice.* Sunderland: University of Sunderland.

Newson, E. (1998) in collaboration with P. Christie and staff of Sutherland House School. *Education and Handling Guidelines for Children with Pathological Demand Avoidance Syndrome.* Nottingham: Elizabeth Newson Centre.

Newson, E. (1999) *The Family of Pervasive Developmental Disorders.* Nottingham: Elizabeth Newson Centre.

Newson, E. and David, C. (1999) 'Pathological Demand Avoidance Syndrome: What Is the Outlook?' In P. Shattock, and G. Linfoot (eds) *From Research into Therapy.* Sunderland: University of Sunderland.

Newson, E. and Le Marechal, K. (1998) 'Pathological Demand Avoidance Syndrome: Discriminate Functions Analysis Demonstrating Its Essential Differences from Autism and Asperger's Syndrome.' In P. Shattock and G. Linfoot (eds) *Psychobiology of Autism: Current Research and Practice.* Sunderland: University of Sunderland.

Newson, E., Le Marechal, K. and David, C. (2000) 'Pathological demand avoidance syndrome: A necessary distinction within the pervasive developmental disorders.' Nottingham: Early Years Diagnostic Centre.

Newson, E., Le Marechal, K. and David, C. (2003) 'Pathological demand avoidance syndrome: A necessary distinction within the pervasive developmental disorders.' *Archives of Disease in Childhood 88*, 7, 595–600.

Newton, C., Taylor, G. and Wilson, D. (1996) 'Circles of friends: An inclusive approach to meeting emotional and behavioural needs.' *Educational Psychology in Practice 11*, 4, 41–48.

Ofsted (2009) *New Framework.* London: Ofsted.

O'Nions, E., Viding, E., Greven, C., Plomin, R. and Happé, F. (in preparation) 'Exploring the construct of pathological demand avoidance: Phenotypic and genetic analyses.'

Power, E. (2010) *Surviving the Special Educational Needs Jungle: Guerrilla Mum.* London: Jessica Kingsley Publishers.

Rosenblatt, M. (2008) *I Exist: The Message from Adults with Autism in England.* London: National Autistic Society.

Row, S. (2005) *Surviving the Special Educational Needs System: How to Be a 'Velvet Bulldozer'.* London: Jessica Kingsley Publishers.

Rutter, M. (ed.) (1971) *Infantile Autism: Concepts, Characteristics and Treatment.* London: Churchill and Sons.

Scott, F.J., Baron-Cohen, S., Bolton, P. and Brayne, C. (2002) 'The CAST (Childhood Asperger Syndrome Test): Preliminary development of a UK screen for mainstream primary-school-age children.' *Autism 6*, 9–31.

Simonoff, E., Pickles, A., Charman, T., Chandler, S., Loucas., T. and Baird, G. (2008) 'Psychiatric disorders in children with autism spectrum disorders: Prevalence, comorbidity, and associated factors in a population-derived sample.' *Journal of the American Academy of Child and Adolescent Psychiatry 47*, 4, 921–929.

Wing, J.K. (ed.) (1966) *Early Childhood Autism.* Oxford: Pergamon Press.

Wing, L. (1971) *Autistic Children: A Guide for Parents.* London: Constable.

Wing, L., Leekam, S., Libby, S., Gould, J. and Larcombe, M. (2002) 'Diagnostic Interview for Social and Communication Disorders: Background, inter-rater reliability and clinical use.' *Journal of Child Psychology and Psychiatry 43*, 307–325.

World Health Organization (1992) *International Statistical Classification of Diseases and Related Health Problems, 10th Revision (ICD-10).* Geneva: WHO.

SUBJECT INDEX

AUTHOR INDEX